Jessie Sale Lloyd

Scamp

Vol. II

Jessie Sale Lloyd

Scamp
Vol. II

ISBN/EAN: 9783337051402

Printed in Europe, USA, Canada, Australia, Japan

Cover: Foto ©ninafisch / pixelio.de

More available books at **www.hansebooks.com**

Jessie Sale Lloyd

Scamp
Vol. II

ISBN/EAN: 9783337051402

Printed in Europe, USA, Canada, Australia, Japan

Cover: Foto ©ninafisch / pixelio.de

More available books at **www.hansebooks.com**

SCAMP.

A NOVEL.

BY

J. SALE LLOYD,

AUTHOR OF

"SHADOWS OF THE PAST," "RUTH EVERINGHAM,"
"WE COSTELIONS," "THE SILENT SHADOW," "GOLD AND SILVER."
ETC., ETC.

IN THREE VOLUMES.

VOL. II.

LONDON:
F. V. WHITE & CO.,
31 SOUTHAMPTON STREET, STRAND, W.C.

1887.

[All Rights reserved.]

EDINBURGH
COLSTON AND COMPANY
PRINTERS.

CONTENTS.

CHAP.		PAGE
I.	Sir Richard's Birthday Gift to Lilian,	1
II.	Sir Richard puzzles the Lawyer,	25
III.	The Mystery solved,	54
IV.	"Oh, Cecil, Cecil, how You have made Me suffer!"	80
V.	"Good-bye,"	103
VI.	Seen through a Leafy Screen,	128
VII.	"I could not give You Love for Love,"	154
VIII.	A Last Look at the Rosy West,	180
IX.	The New Rector of Winsthorpe,	193
X.	Sir Richard's Ruse,	218

EIGHT POPULAR NOVELS.

Now ready, in One Vol., the Seventh Edition of

ARMY SOCIETY; or, Life in a Garrison Town. By JOHN STRANGE WINTER. Author of 'Bootles' Baby.' Cloth gilt, 6s.; also picture boards, 2s.

GARRISON GOSSIP, Gathered in Blankhampton. By the same Author. Cloth gilt, 3s. 6d.

THE OUTSIDER. A Sporting Novel. By HAWLEY SMART. New Edition. In 1 vol.

THE GIRL IN THE BROWN HABIT. A Sporting Novel By Mrs EDWARD KENNARD. Cloth gilt, 3s. 6d.

STRAIGHT AS A DIE. By the same Author. Cloth gilt, 3s. 6d.

BY WOMAN'S WIT. By Mrs ALEXANDER. Author of 'The Wooing O't.' Cloth gilt, 3s. 6d.

KILLED IN THE OPEN. By Mrs EDWARD KENNARD. Author of 'The Right Sort.' Cloth gilt, 3s. 6d.

IN A GRASS COUNTRY. By Mrs H. LOVETT-CAMERON. Author of 'A North Country Maid,' etc. (Sixth Edition.) Cloth gilt, 3s. 6d.

F. V. WHITE & Co., 31 Southampton Street, Strand, London, W.C.

SCAMP.

CHAPTER I.

SIR RICHARD'S BIRTHDAY GIFT TO LILIAN.

HORACE LAKE was standing upon the colossal steps of Marsden Hall, waiting for the great clock over the lofty archway leading to the stables to strike the half-hour past eight, before laying his hand upon the mediæval bell-pull, to summon the solemn butler to admit him to the mansion. But early as he was, there were two people already in the dining-room prepared to receive him—Sir Richard Freemantle and Adela Thorndyke. The former greeted him with an indifferent nod.

Certainly not as if he had come with his permission, and by his invitation. But Adela's bright face and friendly hand-clasp reassured him; moreover, he noticed the breakfast-table was laid for four.

"You must humour all Sir Richard's whims," whispered Adela, and turned aside quickly from Horace, that her host should not see them in conversation.

And he nodded to show his comprehension of her instructions.

"You cannot see Lilian until she has received my present," remarked Sir Richard at length to his matutinal visitor; "so perhaps you will be good enough to go behind that screen, young gentleman, and seat yourself in the chair there placed for you; and I shall be obliged by your neither moving nor speaking until I give you permission," and he pointed to a fourfold Japanese screen of black, richly embroidered in gold, some six feet high.

"Come along, Horace," said Adela, with a bright smile. "What fun! how delighted our dear girl will be to see you under her father's roof."

"Am I really to understand, sir, that you have consented to Lilian's becoming my wife?" asked the young lawyer, with agitation.

"Understand what you please," grumbled the Baronet. "Old folks always have to give way in the end."

"Thank you! thank you a thousand times," began Horace; but Sir Richard waved his thanks aside. "Go to your chair, Mr Lake; and mind, not a word, not a sound!"

"You shall be obeyed, sir," he replied readily.

"Then look out of that window all the time, Horace," whispered Adela; and as she stood beside him she deftly pinned a placard on his back unknown to him, with the pretence of brushing something from his coat.

"Come, Sir Richard, and see if that position will do," she laughed; and in another moment the Baronet was by her side, and the chuckle which Horace had heard several times the previous day was audibly repeated.

"Capital! capital! You always know just what I want, my dear!" he said warmly.

The thought occurred to Horace Lake that Adela had not much to do with the position he had taken up, but since it gave Lilian's father satisfaction to think she had, the pleasant delusion could not affect *him* in any way.

The whole transaction, however, was

very strange, and he thought Sir Richard must be getting a little childish, to wish him to sit behind a screen while he gave his daughter his birthday present.

But Adela had said that he was to be humoured, so of course he must be. The little farce would soon be over, and it would not hurt him at all, as he was not invited to perform in it. If he had been, he would gladly have taken any part assigned to him, to draw him nearer to Lilian, and win her father's favour; for although he did not doubt she would marry him, even in defiance of his wishes, still he knew but too well that it would be a cloud over her happiness, to feel that she had reached it by the paths of disobedience.

"Here is to-day's paper for you, Mr Lake," said Sir Richard quietly, as though it were quite an everyday occurrence to hide people behind screens.

"Thank you, sir, but I could not read, I could not concentrate my thoughts; you forget I'm to see Lilian presently."

"Not a bit of it; but what's the use of wasting time? You'll get through the leading articles if you're a brisk reader."

But Horace again declined the paper, and followed Adela's instruction to look out of the window.

. . . .

At that momont something happened which none of them had anticipated. Lilian's sweet voice was heard in the distance singing "Love's Request."

> "Stay with me, my darling, stay,
> And like a dream thy life shall pass away."

The great gong clanged out the announcement that breakfast was ready, and the solemn butler noiselessly brought in the tea and coffee, and the hot dishes, and placed them on the table.

But instead of coming into the room, the singer passed along the hall, and ran out into the keen morning air, to gather, for her own decoration, a bunch of red chrysanthemums, and one of white for Adela.

"Not a word, sir," whispered the Baronet.

"Don't move, old chap!" said Adela; "she'll be here directly."

And Horace sat looking out of the window.

Suddenly Lilian passed.

Involuntarily he started.

All at once she glanced in, and their eyes met.

He laid his finger upon his lips to enjoin silence, and with a joyous laugh the girl came dashing into the house.

"Dear old Dela!" she murmured. "This is her surprise in honour of my birthday! She knows papa never appears downstairs till one o'clock."

She rushed into the room wildly.

"You dear old girl!" she cried, clasping her arms about her friend's neck.

"How good you are! But what would papa say if he found out?"

"Hush!" whispered Adela, and made a motion with her hand towards the further end of the room, where sat Sir Richard, with the newspaper in his hands, well up before his face.

Lilian uttered a cry of alarm.

"Hallo! what on earth is the matter?" he inquired, not understanding the cause of her agitation, and little dreaming of the apparition she had beheld through the window.

"Nothing, papa, nothing," she answered uneasily.

Then turning to her friend she whispered with much agitation,—

"Oh! Dela, darling! *Can't* you open that window, and let Horace out? It was very kind of you; but it was too great a risk. Oh! what *will* papa do to Horace? I'm sure he will horsewhip him!"

"Hush!" returned the other; "be quiet, Lil."

In the meantime Sir Richard had got himself out of the depths of his easy chair, and was approaching his daughter somewhat feebly, but with a kind and affectionate smile upon his handsome old face. And Lilian told herself that it was evident *he* did not dream of her disobedience, or that Adela had been a traitor in his camp, and had admitted his enemy."

"My dear child!" he said, gently; "you are surprised not only to see me up, but to find me down, I am sure."

"I am indeed, papa!" she faltered.

"It is in honour of your birthday, Lilian," he continued. "I feel I have somewhat neglected it hitherto, and I am going to begin a new era to-day."

"No, no, papa, you have never neglected it! I have many kind birthday gifts of yours!" she replied earnestly.

"A few poor trifles, but I don't remember that I ever tried to do anything to make the day a landmark in your life. I never did anything to make you feel the happier for being a year older, I am sure."

"You are very kind!" she answered simply.

"I want to be, my dear," he said, with feeling; "and I have a great deal to say to you; but I have invited a friend to breakfast, so I must be brief."

"Oh! papa, you will quite overtire yourself coming down so early. Shall I not breakfast with you upstairs?"

"No, no; you forget my friend!"

"I did, I confess!"

She glanced helplessly towards Adela, but for once she seemed to have deserted her, and would not meet her anxious eyes. Never before had Lilian felt so vexed with her.

"Never before had Adela so mismanaged everything," thought the poor girl; and the feeling came into her mind, that, instead of a *happy* birthday, it was likely to prove the most miserable one she had ever spent.

"Before we begin breakfast, Lilian," continued Sir Richard, with feeling, "I must give you my offering upon this festive occasion. Yes, my dear, I hope you will think the phrase aptly chosen—*this festive occasion*," he chuckled. "At the same time I must confess that it has cost me a good deal to do it,—more than you will realise, perhaps, for I had made other plans, I fear. But Adela has helped me in the arrangement of my gift; she knows your tastes better than I do, so I hope you will be satisfied, my dear. Accept it with my affectionate love, Lilian! *You will find it behind the screen!*"

"Behind the screen!"

Poor Lilian gave an hysterical cry.

"Oh, thank you, father; I am sure to like it!" she said.

But she never moved an inch.

"What! are you too lazy to look after your own present? I would fetch it for you, my dear, but it is too heavy: I couldn't lift it."

Adela was making signs to her to go behind the screen, and her father's next words decided her.

"My dear, we must go together if you won't go alone."

She glanced appealingly at her friend.

"Oh, stop him!" she whispered, and rushed forward.

In front of her sat Horace Lake, looking out of the window, and on his back, little as he was aware of the fact, was a placard bearing these words in large letters,—

"A birthday present to my dear daughter Lilian, from her affectionate father,
    "RICHARD FREEMANTLE."

And the signature was in the Baronet's own handwriting.

"Oh, papa, have you really, really given me to Horace?" she cried.

"No, my dear; I have given *him* to *you!*" said her father, with emotion, coming to her side, and kissing her with real feeling. "And now, young man, it is *your* turn," he added, and wheeling sharply round, he seated himself at the table. "Come, Adela," he said; "we're out of it. We may as well have our breakfast.

It is fortunate hot-water dishes have been invented, or our cutlets would not be eatable."

But there was a look of happiness in his face, and a moisture in his keen eyes, unusual to either, notwithstanding his commonplace words.

"Lilian, my heart's darling, mine indeed now!" whispered Horace Lake, as he clasped the agitated girl to his breast. "Your father has been very kind, dearest; he has put aside his own wishes, and has consented to our union."

"Oh, Horace! can it be true?" she gasped.

"Quite, quite true, dearest," he answered joyously. "No more hidden meetings, no more surreptitious letters, no more Mercury business for dear old Scamp. We may own our love before the world, my darling, now. There is only one reservation on your father's part—if you marry me you will not be his heiress. Will you make that sacrifice for my sake, pet?"

"Will I not!" she returned reassuringly. "If I have no money, Horace, no one can say you married me for it, can they?"

"No, indeed, little one. I should be sorry if they could. How proud I shall be to work for you, my own!"

She looked happily up into the animated face.

"I never dreamed that papa would be so kind," continued she at length.

"Nor I. It is all dear old Scamp's doing."

"Did she coax papa into it?"

"There is not the least doubt of it."

"Then I wonder no longer. Scamp could do anything! With her gentle, saucy ways she would win gold from a miser, love from a misanthrope, or charity from a parson!"

He laughed.

"What would her father say at the expression of such an opinion, Lilian?" asked her lover.

"He has heard it before, Horace."

"There is plenty of charity in the Rector of Winsthorpe to count in the scale against a number of detrimentals."

"There is, indeed. He is a man in a hundred, and a parson in a thousand."

"Your opinion of them is not elevated, then?"

"No; they preach much, and practice little. I am glad you are not one of them."

"According to Sir Richard's ideas, lawyers are *all* rascals!" he said amusedly.

"That is very likely. I don't object to that so much—it is their trade to make wrong appear right; but what I hate is to see wrong things done under the cloak of religion!"

"There you are quite right, dear; and now, my pet, I want to be selfish, and talk of ourselves. My dear girl, I do most heartily hope this may be a bright and happy year to you. When I bought this," he continued, slipping a gipsy ring set with brilliants from his waistcoat pocket, "I had no thought that you would be able to wear it for the next two years; but now, love, I shall place it upon its right and proper finger. We must take it off just once, dear, to put on a plain golden fetter, and then it can go back again for ever. You will wear it for my sake, Lilian?"

"While life lasts," she answered earnestly, and he once more held her in his arms in a close embrace. "It is lovely!" she said brightly, looking at her ring.

"And now shall I show it to papa, Horace?"

"By all means, if you like."

"Oh! there you are!" exclaimed Sir Richard, as they emerged from their hiding-place. "I was beginning to think you understood my invitation to be to lunch, Mr Lake."

"Have we been so very long, sir? It did not seem so to me."

"I daresay not," and again that chuckle was most audible.

"I have to thank you for your goodness, and Adela for her championship," began Horace, when the Baronet interrupted him.

"Don't you think you had better wait, young gentleman? Breakfast is decidedly cold already, and I have quite finished. Adela, my dear, I have some letters to answer. Will you do them for me?"

"Willingly," she replied at once.

"Then we will make ourselves scarce. "I won't refuse your arm, my dear, if you like to offer it."

"Of course I like to offer it," she returned kindly, and suited the action to the word.

"Papa! I *must* tell you how grateful I am," whispered Lilian, clinging to his other arm.

"*Don't*, my dear; I never could stand thanks. The anticipation of them has many a time prevented my doing a good action."

"Well! I *am* grateful!" she returned, with tears of happiness in her eyes, "whether I may express my feelings or no."

"All right, my dear; I suppose you know your own mind."

"Indeed I do."

"Ah! so did I—so did I. Adela, my dear, I am ready."

"Oh! papa, I *must* show you my ring. Is it not pretty?"

"Very nice, very nice. Soon got the

fetters riveted—eh! young man? Well, well, youth is always in haste, and age is slow! Very odd, very odd, when one has a long life before him, and the other may count it by days. I suppose I shall see you at lunch, Mr Lake?" he added, with a grim smile.

"Thank you very much, sir, if I may be permitted."

"If not, I should then have said plainly, 'I wish you good day, young man, as I shall *not* see you at lunch.' You need never mistake my meaning unless you choose," and the old man went off chuckling upon Adela's arm.

"You are rather tired, are you not, Sir Richard?" she asked kindly.

"A little, my dear. But I must begin to look up my strength for our journey to the land of frogs."

"You must, indeed."

"I'll take you to Paris, my dear;

it is the best capital in the world for amusing yourself. You have never been there, have you?"

"Never; but you must get better before you think of our pleasures; and now, will you rest on the sofa while I write?"

"Thank you, lassie, so I will; I like to watch you."

She gave him a bright glance, wrapped him up, arranged his pillows, and set out her writing materials, waiting for his instructions, pen in hand.

"What shall I do without you, Adela?" he said thoughtfully, his eyes resting upon her sadly. "At latest, when the winter is over, your father will want you back at the Rectory."

"You will have Lilian," she replied gently. "She will have learnt before then how dear you are to each other!"

"She will never understand my ways as you do, my dear."

"Oh! I hope so. The light of love will have taught her how to please you!"

"And when she is married?"

"That will not be for two years, and no one knows what may happen before then!"

"You may have found a sweetheart too—eh, Pussy?"

The hot blood mantled her cheek, then left her paler than before.

"You are not likely to hear that," she answered gravely, and the hand that held the pen trembled.

"Forgive me, child!" he said earnestly. "I did not mean to pain you; but you are too young to wear the willow for any man. You will get over it in time, Adela; it is not as when two lives have *grown together*, and taken deep root!"

"The heart knoweth its own bitterness," she answered, with a sad smile. "No one can judge of the powers of loving or suffering of another. As for the willow, dear friend, I do *not* wear it. If I mourn, it is in spirit only. To the world I am the same as ever, Adela Thorndyke, the Scamp!"

"Well, well! I wish I could make *you* happy as easily as I have done Lilian. I would if it cost me my estate, believe me!"

"I am sure of it," she replied, with feeling.

"We managed capitally this morning, my dear!" he said, changing the subject with tact.

"We did, indeed!" she answered, a smile chasing away the clouds.

"I could not quite understand why Lilian was so slow in going to look after my gift!" he went on, in a puzzled way.

Adela's laughter rang out.

"I daresay not," she returned; and then she told him how Lilian had seen Horace from the garden, and thought he was there without *his* knowledge, and her horror, when she found both lover and father in the same room, divided only by a screen, and explained her anxiety to get the one out of the window, and the other out of the door, back to his own chamber.

The humour of the situation suddenly struck the old man, and he laughed till the tears trickled down his lined face, and Adela laughed too, as though there was no Cecil Egerton in the world.

CHAPTER II.

SIR RICHARD PUZZLES THE LAWYER.

WHEN Sir Richard and Adela went down to luncheon there was no need for them to inquire whether Lilian had spent a pleasant morning, for her face was radiantly bright.

She and Horace had, however, really been too long engaged, although without parental sanction, to obtrude their feelings upon others, when the first astonishment and joy was over; and only a few fond and trustful glances told they were lovers.

Both were in the best of spirits, and their cheerfulness was contagious, and soon the conversation became sparkling and animated, and the Baronet ceased to wonder at his daughter's choice, as he listened to Horace's amusing sallies, and looked at his handsome face.

A pang of regret shot through his mind at his want of position in the county, but he thrust it back impatiently, and determined to try and overcome his aristocratic prejudices.

"What are you young people going to do this afternoon?" he asked at length.

"Suppose you all three drive over to the Rectory, and tell our good friends there your little bit of news — eh! Lilian?"

"I should like it so much, papa. I know both Mr and Mrs Thorndyke will be really glad, although they would not encourage me in disobedience," she returned, with a smile.

"As Adela did," laughed the Baronet.

"Oh! you must not say that, papa; no one knows how good Dela has been to me."

"Oh yes! he may," cried Scamp brightly. "He may say whatever he likes. It is *he* who is good, really good; for he has overcome himself. There is no merit in standing by a friend."

"Who helped me?" inquired Sir Richard, looking at Adela.

"Your own kind heart," she said softly.

He was about to deny it, when she struck in with her sweet, imperious way,—

"I *won't* be contradicted, Sir Richard, so you had better give in at once."

"Very well," he answered merrily; "but I shall punish you by staying abroad a month longer than I meant to do."

"Abroad! Surely you are not going away, papa?" asked Lilian, looking up.

"Yes, my dear. The doctor has ordered me to leave England at once."

"Oh! papa! I am so sorry."

"Sorry! Why?"

"I shall miss you greatly," she answered, with feeling.

"Not a bit of it; you are coming too. You would not have me go alone, would you?"

"Oh! no, papa!" she said hesitatingly, with her eyes downcast and her colour deepening. "Of course you cannot go alone; it was thoughtless of me to imagine it for a moment. Indeed I shall be very glad to go and take care of you."

"I can't say you looked very overjoyed, my dear!" he answered grimly.

"Naturally I wish we could all have remained here, especially now that we are going to be so happy."

"Speak for yourself, my dear, speak for yourself. I see before *me* a very barren life! That young rascal promised me the next two years of your society without his interference, and he has been poaching all the morning. Well, Lilian, tell the truth—you don't like to leave your lover?"

"No, papa, I don't."

"Well, I will go without you."

"Not for the world. Horace can do without me better than you can now, father, for you are not well."

A smile of satisfaction lighted up his face, which was reflected upon Adela's, who gave him a glance, as much as to say, "I told you so."

"And what do you say to the arrangement, young gentleman?" demanded the Baronet, turning suddenly upon Horace.

"Lilian has given the right decision, sir," he replied; "she must certainly accompany you."

The smile deepened.

"You two will want to write love-letters to each other, I suppose," he remarked, with a wicked twinkle in his eyes. "I conclude I must consent to it once a month or so!"

"A little oftener than that I hope, sir," pleaded Horace.

"Never satisfied!" he laughed. "Well, I must see! I'll think about it, Lake."

Then he turned to Lilian.

"We must coax the Rector to let Adela accompany us, my dear; we could not do without her yet, could we?"

"Oh! Dela, I am more than glad. If only Horace were going too, how I should enjoy it!"

And a silence followed her remark.

Two of them knew that he *was* to go,

but the Baronet liked to let out his favours in surprises, and Adela had no mind to thwart his whim.

Lilian's wish was expressed upon the impulse of the moment, with no thought of the possibility of such a scheme.

Horace gave her a grateful glance, but shook his head.

"How would my work get on, little one? No, there must be no pleasure-making for me for the next two years," he answered, in a very low voice; "then I will take my dear girl abroad myself, and how I shall enjoy it!"

Their eyes met, and their hands met furtively, too, under the table.

"I *have* communicated with the Rector on the subject, and all you have to do this afternoon is to bring me his consent to Adela's accompanying us," said the Baronet.

"We will not both leave you," said

Adela hastily; "let Lilian and Horace go over together, dear Sir Richard."

"Without a *chaperon!* Impossible. No, my dear girl, you must do Gooseberry, and I'll take a nap. By-the-bye, bring the Rector and his good wife back to dinner."

"That *would* be nice!" replied Adela warmly.

"And tell them the carriage shall take them home in the evening."

"How thoughtful you are!"

"Am I? Then I must have learnt the trick of you, missy," he laughed. "Now, girls, go and dress. Suppose you help me upstairs, Master Horace. I think your hair will want smoothing before you appear in respectable society. Have you looked at yourself in the glass lately?"

"Not since I made it all stand on end as far as I could," laughed Lilian; "but it is so curly, and I cannot succeed very well."

"What things you girls are!" grumbled Sir Richard. "What a way to show your affection for a man, to try and make his hair stand on end! One would think you wanted him for a bottle brush! Go on, the pair of you, or Adela will be trying her pranks on me to keep you in countenance."

And as he spoke he took Horace by the arm, and led him from the room.

"Well!" he said, when they were alone, "Lilian's birthday only comes once a year. I suppose you want to stay to dinner. I'll send over for your clothes."

"That is indeed kind of you, sir. With your permission I will write a note to my mother, and tell her what to pack up for me. They do not even know where I am to-day."

"Bad son! bad son!" returned the old man, with pretended deprecation.

"I left a message to say I could not

tell when I should be back," continued Horace.

"Oh! of course, of course! Trying to take off the unfavourable impression, eh?"

Horace laughed.

"Well, sir, I cannot pretend to desire your *un*favourable opinion," he admitted.

"Well, then, make my child happy," said Sir Richard gravely, "and you will deserve my good one."

"It shall not be my fault, sir, if sorrow reaches my dear girl. I will shield her from it, Heaven helping me," he replied earnestly.

In silence Sir Richard clasped the young man's hand.

"May *He* bless you in your endeavour," he answered brokenly, after a pause. "May Lilian be as dear to you as her mother was to me."

Then he turned from him abruptly,

and Horace went out with quiet steps, and left him alone.

When Adela and Lilian came in to say "Good-bye," they found him very still.

"Send Harvey to me, Lilian," he said, and his valet entered the room as they went downstairs.

"I am going to write a note," he asserted. "Order the dogcart round, and when it is prepared, you are to come back to me for instructions. Just ask Mr Lake if his letter is ready before he starts."

The man found it already in the hands of the butler, and informed his master of the fact, also that the trap was at the door, a quarter of an hour later.

"Very well, take this note and Mr Lake's; leave the latter at Mr Lake's house, and say you will return for Mr Horace's bag. Then drive on to the office, and bring Mr Lake back with you, after giving him my letter. Remember you are not to return without him, and you are to call for the bag on your way. Do you understand?"

"Perfectly, Sir Richard."

"Tell the groom to drive quickly, I want to see Mr Lake as soon as possible."

"I beg your pardon, sir, I hope you are not feeling worse," began the man anxiously.

"Don't trouble yourself, Harvey; my will was made long ago, if I make another it won't be in a hurry."

"No offence, sir, I hope. I humbly beg your pardon."

"Don't waste time, man, go at once."

The valet withdrew with a respectful bow, and in less than five minutes Sir Richard was asleep.

Great indeed was the astonishment at

Mr Lake's residence, when the Baronet's dogcart dashed up to the door, and Horace's note was placed in his mother's hand.

"Dear Mumsy," it ran,—"Send me over all my dinner toggery in my small portmanteau by the bearer, please. I have *so* much to tell you, but it must keep till we meet. One thing, however, I must say, and that is, there never was a happier fellow than your loving son,

"Horace."

Mrs Lake sat looking at the lines in bewilderment.

What did it all mean?

There never was a happier fellow than her son Horace!

Her motherly heart gave a great bound of gladness, for there had been moments when her boy's bright and handsome face had been sad indeed.

"The young man said he would be back for the bag in a few minutes," ventured the abigail.

Mrs Lake started.

"Of course, Fanny, I will select the things at once," and she did so, her mind still upon her son's words.

Mr Lake was perfectly aware that he and Sir Richard Freemantle were *two*, both as friends and acquaintances, as well as in a business point of view.

He had managed a good many matters for him in days gone by, before Horace had presumed to love his daughter, but that time was over, and no communication had passed between the Hall and the solicitor's house or office since.

He was therefore bewildered to hear that Sir Richard Freemantle's dogcart was waiting to convey him to Marsden Hall, with the request that he would kindly start as soon as possible.

Moreover a note was placed in his hand, written by the Baronet himself.

"Sir Richard Freemantle presents his compliments to Mr Lake, and will be obliged by his coming to see him at once, upon *pressing business.*"

The lawyer called for his hat and overcoat. The Baronet was not a client to be kept waiting.

It was evident he was to receive some instructions, possibly to be taken into favour again, and the law management of the Marsden Hall estates was worth having.

So Mr Lake went willingly, and with all speed.

He had not forgotten Sir Richard's bitter words to him, but he could afford to put them aside, if it were to his advantage to do so.

He looked surprised when the dogcart stopped at his house, and the valet sprang down from the back seat to ring the bell. His own maid quickly answered it, with his son's small portmanteau in her hand.

"Misses says can you come in and speak to her, sir?" she asked.

"Not now, Fanny, but I shall soon be home, tell Mrs Lake. Where is that going?"

"Please, sir, I don't know; this gentleman said he would call for it."

And she pointed to Harvey the valet.

"I am following Sir Richard's instructions," replied the man.

And slipping the portmanteau under the seat, he again jumped up.

The high-mettled horse dashed forward at a brisk trot, and in a very few minutes they had left the town, and had traversed the intervening two miles which divided them from Marsden Hall.

Sir Richard was still asleep when Harvey opened the door, entering the room with the solicitor behind him.

"Hullo! wouldn't come, you say!" he cried, starting up.

"Mr Lake is here, sir," returned the man.

And that personage stepped forward, while the valet retired.

"You don't often catch me napping, Mr Lake," said the Baronet, with a grim smile. "I have been an invalid lately, so I must be excused."

"Certainly," began the other politely, "a siesta in the afternoon is often very refreshing. I am sorry you have been in ill-health. We have not met for some time."

"No, not since your young rascal of a son chose to make love to my daughter, and what's more, sir, he's at it still, at this very moment!"

Mr Lake's hopes went down.

Instead of being reinstated as the Baronet's man of business, had he been sent for to hear again of Horace's enormities? It seemed very like it.

"It is a matter of regret to me, Sir Richard, that my son should do anything to annoy you. My only excuse for him is, that I am sure he and the young lady are sincerely attached to each other; but believe me, I do nothing to encourage it; on the contrary, I *dis*courage it!"

"Then why not send the rogue abroad for a time?" he asked sharply.

"Impossible! I could not afford it, sir."

"Tut—tut—that shall not stand in his way. Look here, Lake, I have a little business to be done at Mentone; let the lad go there for the winter months."

"But, sir, I should have to engage another clerk in his place."

"Yes, *pro tem.*, and you can charge his salary in my bill, also that of Master Horace; the two combined won't ruin me."

"I don't like to decide without speaking to my son: he may not wish to go."

"Give him the chance," chuckled the Baronet; "if he says no, let there be an end of the matter."

"You cannot speak more handsomely than that, Sir Richard," returned Mr Lake warmly. "Horace ought to consider himself a lucky fellow to have the opportunity of getting such a trip. You specified Mentone, I think, as his place of residence!"

"I did, but I have no objection to his having a look at Paris on his way there—not a bit—I should like to do so myself were I in his place."

"You are very kind, sir; and may I ask whether you hope that absence will shake the faith of our children towards each other, for if you propose the arrangement with any such expectations, I think it is only fair to tell you that I do not believe my son Horace will ever change in his affection for Miss Lilian. For the rest, though I shall miss him very much, I should like him to accept your offer. He has fretted a great deal, and the change would do him good; only it would not be honourable in me to hold out any hope that he will give up his suit upon his return."

"We will see, we will see," replied the baronet, with a merry twinkle in his eye, which the man of law failed to understand.

"You will throw no difficulties, then, in the way of the boy's going?"

"None whatever."

"And when can he start?"

"As soon as he will."

"Tut — tut — young people must let their elders settle things for them sometimes; we will say this day week."

"If Horace agrees to the arrangement, most certainly; but I fear he may not like to leave the neighbourhood which holds the girl he loves."

"Romance, nothing but romance."

"Very likely, Sir Richard, but most of us have gone through the phase ourselves, so we must look leniently on these ideas of the young ones."

"Yes, yes, we have all passed through it if we have hearts at all," murmured the old man. "And now, Mr Lake, as we have been friendly over this matter, let us try and work together."

"No one could desire it more than I do, Sir Richard. I am truly sorry any folly of my boy's should have caused you annoyance, but I was powerless to influence him."

"Well, well, all the better; a young man who can't think and act for himself, is not worth much. Suppose you bring Mrs Lake to dinner here to-night, to meet the Rector and his wife? This is my daughter's birthday, and we may as well have a little merry-making."

Mr Lake looked at the baronet in surprise.

"It would be quite like old times," he said hastily, "and Mrs Lake will be highly honoured."

"Then that is settled."

"Thank you, and if I can get hold of Horace, I will sound him about this scheme of yours, Sir Richard, and let you know what he says."

"All right; we dine at seven. Come at half-past six, and you can have a talk with the lad before dinner."

Mr Lake began to think his sometime client was getting a little childish, and the old man was sharp enough to catch his thought in his eye.

"Oh! I forgot to tell you Master Horace will be one of the party," he laughed. "I have asked him to dinner to-night. Even condemned criminals are allowed to say good-bye to their friends, Mr Lake, and I could not be hard on the boy. As you reminded me just now, *we* were young once, and lovers into the bargain."

The lawyer began to feel more than ever puzzled; his mind was so chaotic, he was quite unable to form an opinion upon Sir Richard's seemingly inconsistent conduct. That he should be willing to pay some hundreds of pounds to get rid of a detrimental admirer of his daughter's, and yet so tender of his feelings as to invite him to dinner, to give him the opportunity of saying farewell to the prohibited young lady, were things totally past his comprehension; and very serious fears set in, in his fancy, as to the state of the Baronet's intellect.

"Is there anything I can do for you legally, Sir Richard, before I go?" he asked gravely, "or did you send for me merely to make this proposition, or to give us your kind invitation in person?"

"There is nothing more just now, Lake. We will see how you manage matters with your son," he added cheerily. "If you are successful in your persuasions, there will be a great deal for you to look after this winter, for I *may* be away myself."

Mr Lake looked at him in pity.

Here was Sir Richard wanting to banish Horace, that he might not meet his daughter, and after all he was going away himself. Then a sudden light broke upon the subject. If Lilian was to be left at home alone, there was perhaps some sense in the Baronet's precaution.

"Is not your daughter to accompany you, sir?" he inquired, after a pause.

"That is just as she pleases, Lake; it is the best way to let young people choose for themselves, after all."

"And you do not think she will go?"

"I never said so."

"You had better not let my son have a hint of this, Sir Richard."

"Why?"

"Because he is but human. If Miss Lilian remains here, with no one to protect her from his attentions, is he likely to cease them when she receives them willingly?"

The Baronet chuckled.

"Lawyers are accustomed to have hard nuts to crack, I suppose, Lake. You must do the best you can with the rascal; and now had you not better go, or Mrs Lake may make other arrangements?"

"Just so," he replied, well aware that there would be quite a little domestic commotion on his wife's part at the unexpected invitation, and no end of excitement in the choosing of caps and frills, gloves and laces, for the occasion, and he rose at once.

Sir Richard extended his hand.

"Don't forget, be here at half-past six —dinner will be at seven, then while you are talking to that young rascal of yours, the ladies can tell each other their secrets; it's wonderful how many they find to relate when they get together. For me, if I have one, I keep it to myself. Once told, you never know where it may travel. I don't believe in confidants!"

"It would not do for my clients all to hold your opinions, Sir Richard. Solicitors, like doctors, ought to know the whole of a case if their services are to be of any avail; and in both of our professions we are bound in honour not to reveal what is confided to us."

"In honour, yes! but the article is scarce. A secret is no longer a secret if even your lawyer knows it."

"You have not a very high opinion of—"

"Of *any one*," struck in the Baronet; "all men are ready to look out for their own interests."

"And who would, if they did not?"

"Exactly so. It is every man for himself in this battle of life, and his neighbour, if needs be, for a stepping-stone!

' 'Tis true, 'tis pity; pity 'tis, 'tis true!'

And now Mr Lake, take my dogcart and make use of it; keep it to return in, if madame be not afraid to mount so high."

"She will not object at all, I am sure."

"And the close carriage can leave you as it takes the Rector and his wife home at night. It holds four."

"Thank you, thank you very much."

Sir Richard had once more tucked his legs up on the sofa, and now he laid his head back on the pillow and closed his eyes.

"Good-bye," said Mr Lake.

"Eh! why, you're coming back, are you not?" asked the Baronet irritably.

"Thank you, yes; then '*au revoir*'!"

"Oh certainly, *au revoir* by all means, my good fellow," returned the other, closing his eyes with utter indifference. "You know the way? or touch the bell."

"Thanks, I know my way very well; it is not the first time I have visited you in your room by many."

"Of course not, before that rascal—" began the Baronet, but Mr Lake wouldn't stop for another outbreak against his son, and was quietly closing the door.

"Long-winded fellows those lawyers," grumbled Sir Richard, as he turned on his side. "I've puzzled him anyway,— given him an enigma to work at, which will take him the rest of the afternoon, and then he will not find the answer without help. I've a great mind to tell that young dog the joke, and make him vow that nothing shall take him from the vicinity of Marsden Hall. Then I could storm at his father for an hour." And the old man chuckled till he fell asleep.

CHAPTER III.

THE MYSTERY SOLVED.

"NEVER knew any one so verbose," thought Mr Lake, as he went slowly down the stairs, "and his mental tiles are getting very shaky. How changed from twenty-five years ago, when he brought home his sweet young wife, who worshipped him, although he was twice her age! He was forty then, and how old he looks now; but he cannot be more than sixty-five, aged as he looks. He is wearing badly. I am only his junior by ten years, and I'm a boy compared to him. Poor Sir Richard! What does it all mean?"

"Is the trap to take you home, sir?" asked the butler.

"Yes! and to wait and bring me and Mrs Lake back again," returned the solicitor, with importance. "I'm sorry to give so much trouble."

"Not at all, sir," replied the man politely; and passing out at the door he went to the groom who was in charge of the vehicle, and spoke to him in a low voice.

"I'd better take the horse to the hotel if I have to wait," answered the groom. "All right."

Then Mr Lake jumped up, and was whirled along homeward, with a very preoccupied mind.

"Sir Richard does not seem himself at all," he said to the groom suddenly.

"No, sir, he's very much pulled down.

The *brownkitis* is a very weakening thing," replied the man gravely.

"Yes! illness weakens mind and body," suggested the lawyer.

"It do, sir, but Sir Richard's *mind* is as clear as crystal. He is going away, you know, sir, and he had me in yesterday to give me his orders respecting the 'orses during his absence. Nothink was forgotten, ill as he has been; and I *was* shocked to see him look so thin and white."

"Ah!" replied Mr Lake, and relapsed into silence, feeling more puzzled than before.

Mrs Lake was watching at the window for her husband's arrival, not at all displeased that the outside world should see the good man seated in state in the baronet's handsome trap.

Rumours had crept about of the quarrel between the owner of Marsden Hall and his solicitor.

People had assigned many reasons for it, but the real reason was known only to a few, if guessed by many, for neither the Freemantles nor the Lakes had desired to make the affair the talk of the small town.

The split had been commented upon, was a little nine days' wonder, and now appeared to be forgotten.

Mrs Lake ran to the door to admit her husband.

"Are you going back, sir?" inquired the groom.

"Thank you, we are to be at the Hall at six-thirty. We had better start at a quarter past, I suppose?"

The man touched his hat, and laid his whip gently over the horse's back, and drove to the nearest hotel.

"What's up, I wonder?" he said to himself as he turned into the stable-yard.

Mrs Lake's query was of the same nature,

if not couched in exactly the same language.

"Well, Henry," she asked, with an intent look, "have you good news?"

He walked into the sitting-room, and closed the door.

"I'm blessed if I know," he admitted. "Sir Richard seems to me to be decidedly *cracked*, but that groom of his asserts that he is perfectly clear-headed."

"You didn't ask such a question, surely?"

"Is it likely? One can find out a thing without asking; most people can be *pumped!*"

"Why were you sent for?"

"To invite you and me to dinner, my dear!" he answered, with a smile.

"Us to dinner!" exclaimed the lady, with evident pleasure. "Well, I *am* glad. There is nothing cracked about that, Henry; he wishes to be friends again."

"Just so, but why? It cannot advantage *him* in any way, and he has invited Horace too!"

"Invited Horace! Then that is what his note to me meant. Henry, depend upon it you will see our boy the Baronet's son-in-law yet!" she cried excitedly.

"Nonsense, my dear! You women are always off at a tangent about something. Sir Richard is so anxious to get rid of the lad that he has decided to send him for the winter to Mentone on some pretended business. The scheme will cost him a cool five hundred!"

"Well, he can afford it!"

"I daresay; but where is your dream picture—eh, wife?"

Mrs Lake looked crestfallen.

"I don't understand. What is his object in wanting to send Horace away?"

"Goodness knows, unless he thinks Lord Carruthers is after his daughter.

I hear he has been a good deal at the Hall lately."

"Does Horace know it?" asked Mrs Lake sharply.

"How can I tell what the lad knows or does not? He is not a boy to talk. My dear, you had better go and look out your finery; for one thing *is* certain, at any rate—we are to be at the Hall at half-past six."

"I would have had a new dress if I had only known," said the good woman, with an air of regret. "We so seldom go out in this little place, and when we do, our things are good enough for our company. But I should have wished to look well to-night for Horace's sake. I should not like him to be ashamed of us; and, my dear, your dress coat *is* so rusty, you really must order another."

"In case Sir Richard should honour us again, eh?" laughed Mr Lake. "Well, my dear, we had better wait, and see whether I get the estate work to do as of yore; if not, I should not feel justified in obliging you till the boys are out in life. As to Horace, he would never be ashamed of his father and mother, if they appeared in rags and tatters!"

"Bless the boy!" replied his wife, with tears in her eyes, "you are right, Henry, he never would," and she ran off upstairs to dress, contentedly arraying herself in her well-worn evening costume.

. . . .

Punctually at half-past six the dog-cart drew up before the hall-door at Marsden, and the butler showed Mr and Mrs Lake into the drawing-room, where they found a merry party already assembled.

"Lake, I am very glad it is all right," said the Rector of Winsthorpe, in a low voice, giving him a friendly grasp of the hand.

"Thank you, thank you!" returned the other, not at all certain upon what he was being congratulated, and passed on to greet the rest of the guests.

"Lilian, my dear, Mrs Lake will like to take off her bonnet if you will conduct her upstairs; and you, young gentleman, can show your father into my room," ended Sir Richard, turning to Horace.

Then, as they left the apartment in pairs, he looked at Adela.

He had turned it over again and again in his mind as to what the girl's trouble *could* be; and having come to the conclusion that it could not possibly be anything but a love affair, set his wits to work to unravel the mystery of whom it could be that she cared for in secret; and he could find no one worthy of such an attachment in the neighbourhood but Lord Carruthers.

Under this impression he had been unusually friendly towards the young nobleman, and had given him a warm welcome whenever he had put in an appearance at the Hall.

"Adela, I have another guest coming this evening," he said suddenly.

"Indeed! what a pity! we were just eight. How naughty of you, Sir Richard!"

"Well, my dear, I don't often entertain, and I shall not have the chance of doing it again for some time, so you must forgive me this once. I have long wanted to ask Lord Carruthers to dinner."

Adela coloured, but made no reply, and the old man thought he had found out her secret.

Mr Thorndyke, who had heard the conversation, struck in warmly,—

"I, at any rate, am glad he is coming. Carruthers is a great favourite of mine, and is always a welcome guest at my house."

"Well! I am pleased that some one is satisfied," he laughed; "and now what about Miss Pussy here? Her cough is still troublesome, and Mentone will set her up, to say nothing of my selfish desire to have her with us. You won't say no, will you, Rector?"

"She has been a long while away from home," returned her father, "and her mother and I miss her sadly, but we do not think it would be right in us to consider our own feelings before her good. Do you want to go, Adela?"

She lifted her eyes to his, full of deep affection, and her hand crept into his.

"My feelings are too mixed to analyse,"

she replied; "*you* shall decide for me, father."

There was a pause, and Mr Thorndyke sat looking upon the ground, wrapped in deep thought.

"You shall go, darling," he said, at length, "and may the journey be for your good, as well as that of your friends."

Sir Richard flung up his velvet cap like a schoolboy, in the excitement of his satisfaction.

"My dear," he said, "I will show you the world. You shall enjoy the trip, if it rests with me."

"She has not seen much of it, so far, poor child. Winsthorpe is a somewhat out-of-the-way place for young people, and of late I have felt no inclination for going about: the change will brighten her up."

"I am bright enough, papa," she

laughed, but there was a wistful look in her beautiful eyes.

"By-the-bye, Adela, your father heard from an old friend of yours to-day," said her mother.

"To be sure," struck in the Rector, "from Egerton. He says his uncle—Lord Lynestone, you know—is in a very shaky state, and wants him to come home and see him, and has offered to pay his expenses if he can get leave to do so; so we *may* have a visit from him in your absence, Scamp, to cheer us up."

Sir Richard knew nothing of Major Egerton, and taking no interest in the conversation, was talking to Mrs Thorndyke about the arrangement for the projected trip, and failed to see the pallor grow upon Adela's cheek.

Her first feeling was a sense of wild disappointment that should Cecil revisit

Winsthorpe, she should not be there to welcome him.

Her second was one of deep relief that she should be spared the meeting.

Not only had he left her, and misjudged her in his passionate anger and jealousy, but he had not once sent her a kindly word since he had been away, when that anger must have cooled, when his sense and judgment should have spoken in her favour.

" Pity the old man married," continued the Rector; " had he not done so, Cecil would have had a fine property. As it is, Lord Lynestone wishes him to undertake the guardianship of his son, from the age of twelve to eighteen, personally; and it is about this he is desirous to see him. Before then he is to remain under his mother's care. Egerton says he will come home if he can, but that he shall only be in England a few days."

"Where is Lord Lynestone living?" asked Adela, for the sake of something to say.

"His estate is in Derbyshire, and the scenery around is the most beautiful which England can produce. We might have had a peep at it had the place fallen into Cecil's hands; but he does not say a word as to whether his uncle is at home, or health-seeking elsewhere."

"At home, I should fancy, if he is so feeble," said Adela thoughtfully.

And at that moment Lord Carruthers was announced.

He looked such a perfect gentleman as he entered the room in his evening clothes, and so handsome, that Adela glanced at him in surprise.

Often as she had seen him she had never been struck by his appearance as

The Mystery solved.

she now was, and the greetings over, he secured the vacant seat by her side, and held it in possession.

In the meantime Lilian had thrown her arms round the neck of Horace's mother, and had burst into joyous tears.

"My dear, what is it?" inquired Mrs Lake, holding her to her breast, and patting her back, as though she were soothing an infant.

"Nothing indeed, only I am so happy, and so is Horace," she answered, smiling through her tears. "Papa has been so kind! Oh! dear Mrs Lake, he has really consented to our being married in two years' time!"

"Then no wonder the boy wrote me such a bright note!" returned Mrs Lake, her face like a sunbeam.

"One thing may disappoint you and Mr Lake, perhaps," continued the girl shyly. "I am not to inherit papa's property or money, but of that Horace says he is rather glad than otherwise; he would not like to be dependent upon his wife."

"And quite right too; I admire his spirit. I had not a sixpence when his father married *me*, and no couple could be happier than we have been; but it will be a change for you, my dear, to live on his means."

"Do you think I shall mind that?" asked Lilian softly.

"Not if you love him truly."

"I do love him with all my heart," she answered, with her bright eyes looking straight into those of Horace's mother. "I *do* love him, and I want you to try and care for me for his sake."

"It won't be very difficult, my dear; I was fond of you as a child. Of late years we have not seen each other, but

I have thought kindly of you because you were true to my boy. Yes, dear, I can, and do, and will love you," she answered warmly.

"Thank you very much," returned the girl, in a low voice. "I never had the comfort of a mother's love; I was so young when she died, and I have so often longed for her gentle guidance."

"You will have Horace to guide you now, darling," said Mrs Lake, smoothing the soft dark hair from her brow; "and I will be a mother to you, Lilian, if you will let me," and they sealed the compact with a kiss of sincere affection.

. . . .

While this conversation was being carried on in Lilian's room, another was in progress in Sir Richard's bed-chamber, between Mr Lake and his son.

"This *is* an unexpected surprise to see

you and my mother here, father," said Horace, his handsome face aglow with pleasure.

"Just so, my boy; no one could have been more taken aback than I was when the Baronet sent for me this afternoon."

"What! have you been here before to-day? Then I suppose you know all about everything?"

"I conclude I do."

"And what do you think of it?"

"Well, my opinion, in confidence, is, that the Baronet is *cracked*."

Horace looked at his father blankly.

"Have you heard of his scheme *to get rid of you?*"

"To get rid of *me?*" echoed the son.

"Yes! he is willing to spend at least five hundred pounds for his whim."

Horace Lake turned pale.

The gladness died out of his face, and he

sat down as though all the strength had gone out of him.

"Go on," he said, much agitated. "Let me hear all."

"Why, the long and the short of it is, that he wants to get you out of the way for the winter. I have an idea that he wishes to clear the coast for some one else, and thinks if Lilian does not see you, that she will forget you."

"Lilian forget me!" retorted Horace scornfully. "Never!"

"Well, I can account for his proceedings in no other way. He is willing to pay all expenses if you will ship yourself off to do some pretended business for him abroad."

"But what is his object? He starts himself this day week."

"The deuce he does! That is the day he said *you* were to go. Does Miss Lilian accompany him?"

"Certainly, and Adela Thorndyke too."

"Then he *must* be mad!"

"Heaven forbid, for Lilian's sake! And where am I to go?" asked Horace suddenly.

"Well, queer as the offer is, I should not refuse it if I were you, Horace. You have looked harassed of late, and it will secure you a long rest and a pleasant winter. He wishes you to go to Mentone for some months, but he has no objection to your visiting Paris on your way, and amusing yourself there or elsewhere as well."

"To Mentone!" almost shouted Horace, sunshine bursting out with a sudden beam upon his handsome face, while he sprang to his feet with so rapid a movement as nearly to upset his father. "Dear, dear old man. I see it all now!"

"Do you?" replied his father dryly. "I confess I don't. If I might venture to express an opinion, I should say there is madness in the air at Marsden Hall. I have been a shrewd lawyer for the past thirty years and more, and I can see through most things, but here the atmosphere is too dense for my vision, I must confess. I am sent for as if it were on a matter of life and death; and when I arrive I am asked to send my son away for six months, for no other reason, as far as I can find out, except to humour some ridiculous fancy. Then I am invited to dinner as a sop, and the moment I enter the room the Rector congratulates me upon the dickens knows what, and now *you* have caught the infection too, by Jove!"

Horace bursting out laughing,—

"I don't believe you know, after all. Didn't mother tell you?"

"She said you were delighted at being asked here."

"Of course I am. What else do you know?"

"That you're as cracked as the rest!" replied Mr Lake irritably. "I never was good at riddles; I'm too old to enjoy them by far."

"Dad," said Horace, with a bright and happy face, "if I am at all insane, it is with joy."

"I only see the result; I know nothing of the cause," returned the lawyer; "but if you are sane enough to explain yourself, I confess I shall be glad."

"This is Lilian's birthday," began Horace.

"So her father informed me; we're here in honour of it," snarled Mr Lake.

"Sir Richard, you know, has been ill," continued his son, "and Adela has been nursing him. Under her gentle influence his heart has softened strangely of late."

"It was soft enough twenty-five years

ago, before sorrow soured him," said the lawyer reflectively. "If you wanted a kind action done, Sir Richard Freemantle was the man to apply to."

"I can believe it now," replied Horace earnestly. "A week ago I could not have done so, but yesterday he sent for me, and questioned me, in his would-be rough manner, as to my love for his daughter, who, he told me, would not inherit his property if she married me. I assured him that I wanted nothing with her; that I would rather work for my own wife than let her be beholden to any one else for what she required; and he seemed pleased. He then desired me to call at half-past eight this morning, and when Lilian came down he *gave me to her*, in his own peculiar way, as though the thing were a joke, rather than a serious sacrifice to his pride and prejudice. Then, as it was my dear girl's birthday, he kept me to spend it with her, and at lunch he told us that he is going to Mentone for the winter months."

"*He* is going to Mentone himself!" interrupted Mr Lake.

"Just so, father; and if he has fixed this day week for me to start, he means me to accompany them."

"And he actually *has* consented to your engagement? Well, the world must be coming to an end!"

"It is just beginning for me, dad. I have often thought myself happy before, but to-day I have really begun to live; and now that you do understand, father, let me hear that you are pleased."

"For your sake, I am; very much so, my boy," replied his father kindly; "although for my own I would rather you had chosen a wife from our own set. Miss Lilian is a very nice girl, but she will miss her grand style of life when she comes to inhabit a lath-and-plaster villa."

" Lilian is the truest girl on earth."

"No doubt she loves you, but she is not likely to be much of a daughter to people with our quiet ways."

" You don't know her," replied his son. " She will love my home and my parents, all for my sake, father. Have no fear about her whatever."

"Then, my boy, you have won a treasure."

" I have," answered Horace gladly, and father and son clasped hands as the gong sounded for dinner, and both hastened downstairs.

CHAPTER IV.

"OH, CECIL, CECIL, HOW YOU HAVE MADE ME SUFFER!"

"E are nine," said Sir Richard, letting his eyes glance around upon his guests. "Rector, you are my oldest and best friend; I can take a liberty with *you*. Will you give me a strong arm, and that will enable me to offer my weak one to Mrs Lake? We three old folks can hobble along together, and the younger ones must follow us. Lord Carruthers, will you take Miss Thorndyke? Mrs Thorndyke will not quarrel with Mr

Lake. And you two, my dears, require no pairing."

Lord Carruthers had heard nothing of the engagement, and gave a glance of surprise at Horace and Lilian under his eyelashes; but the party were on the move, and no explanation was given.

The dinner was a very *recherché* one, for the baronet had arranged the *menu* himself, to the astonishment of his housekeeper, and every one seemed thoroughly to enjoy it.

The guests were glad to be there, and were not ashamed to show their pleasure.

Sir Richard felt happier than he had done for years, and exerted himself to be a good and agreeable host.

Lilian was bright as a summer sky, with her lover by her side, and Adela was purely happy in the joy of others.

Lord Carruthers was well contented with

his position, and was devoting himself to her amusement.

The conversation very naturally ran upon the proposed visit to Mentone, with which place Lord Carruthers was well conversant, and able to give full information as to the best hotels to be found there, etc., and Sir Richard grew greatly interested in all he said.

"You had better come and be our cicerone. Strange if we should all find ourselves there before the winter is out!" he laughed.

"*I* cannot leave my flock," replied Mr Thorndyke, shaking his head.

"Nor I my clients," remarked the lawyer.

"No! but you will both be represented by your children. Carruthers has neither fold nor clients, and nothing on earth to do but amuse himself. He ought to try and be of use to his friends."

His lordship's eyes turned towards Adela, but hers were fixed upon a slice of delicious ice pudding; and no wonder, for it looked uncommonly good.

Had they been raised, however, he would have seen that there was a touch of annoyance in their expression, which did not bespeak any pleasure at the proposition; nor could Sir Richard see them, and he was honestly endeavouring to put things right for her.

He had heard a whisper of his lordship's rejection in days gone by, and his belief was that *having* rejected him she thought him now beyond recall, and was fretting at the fact.

He had, therefore, been watching his visitor for some time past, and had come to the conclusion that Lord Carruthers still loved Adela, and was ready to come forward again upon the faintest encouragement on her part; and he determined to try and throw them together.

"I *shall* be travelling in France and Italy," replied his lordship, with as much carelessness as he could assume; "and very possibly I may look you up at Mentone, since you promise me a welcome."

"We shall all be very pleased to have your company," returned the Baronet decidedly.

But Adela never raised her eyes.

The Rector felt vexed with her, but knew that any word of his would only draw attention to his daughter's silence; so he wisely held his peace, merely expressing his pleasure that Adela would have so many English friends about her to keep home green in her memory.

The dessert had been handed round by the noiseless, well-mannered servants, who, when their duties were done, as quietly withdrew.

The Baronet looked over his shoulder to see that the coast was clear, then turned towards his daughter.

"Speeches," he said, "have long been laid on the shelf with many other pleasant old-world customs; but to-night, my friends, I must claim the privilege of saying a few words in honour of my daughter's birthday, and also engrafted on to that, her betrothal day. Lilian, my love to you, and may you be happy with the man of your choice. I like to have the last word, my dear, so don't let that young thief who has stolen you from me say a number of pretty things he does not mean. One man's gain generally consists in another man's loss."

He let his eyes rest upon her kindly, and raising a bumper to his lips, emptied it in her honour.

A buzz of congratulation followed the Baronet's announcement, by which it was most plainly evident to all, that his opposition was totally withdrawn, and that henceforth Horace was to be received as a future member of the family at Marsden Hall.

Mr Lake no longer thought his client fit for Bedlam; the fog had cleared away, and he felt very proud as he sat there at Sir Richard's well-appointed table, in the reflected light of his son's new honours.

"I am sorry you will not allow me to thank you, Sir Richard," said Horace, with feeling; "but all the dictionary strung together could never express the gratitude I feel, believe me!"

"Yes! yes! You have got your own way, lad. It is wonderful how amiable people are when they have all they want! I know I am myself."

"Does that happy stage of existence ever arrive really?" asked Lord Carruthers, with a smile.

"It did with me," replied the Baronet, in a low voice, with a far-off look; "but it was too bright to last. We should need no heaven if it were to do so."

And they all knew that the perfect happiness he referred to, had been found in the wife of his love; and his words threw a solemn silence upon them.

. . . .

"Father," said Horace, as he drew Mr Lake aside into a quiet corner of the spacious drawing-room, "I had not time to ask you what you meant about its costing Sir Richard five hundred pounds for me to go to Mentone!"

"Well, my boy, he has promised to pay your salary while you are there and that of some one else to do your work *pro tem.*, and he will of course consider you his guest during your stay."

"I could not accept it," returned Horace firmly.

"What! don't you want to go?" asked Mr Lake in astonishment.

"More than anything. But neither you nor I could play such an unhandsome part."

"I don't quite see that."

"Don't you? then *I* do. I could not make money out of Lilian's father!"

"I don't look at it in that light. It is a business transaction.

"Nonsense, father! there is no business about it; had there been, it would have been all right. So long as you did not know of the existing relations between us you were not to be blamed for entertaining the idea; but now the thing is impossible."

"What do you propose, then?"

"Bob would undertake my work for me, I'm certain."

"Your brother is very good-natured; I daresay he would. You can ask him, at any rate."

"I'll get *some one* to stand in the gap; and as to my own salary—I'll do without it."

"You're rather Quixotic! You'll offer to pay Sir Richard for your board next."

"Not I! I should be sorry to insult him."

"I didn't know how far your pride might carry you," returned Mr Lake snappishly.

"Father! you know I am right."

And the lawyer *did* know it, and that *he* was wrong, and for that very reason he felt out of humour with his son for making him feel the fact.

Sir Richard had not once remained

in the drawing-room to listen to music since the voice of the woman he idolised had ceased to fill it with rich melody. Now he walked to the fine old grand piano, and opened it himself.

His daughter's voice and musical talent had been well cultivated at his desire; but when she sang he had shut himself away from the sound of her music as far as he could; and, knowing this, Lilian had entirely given up singing when he was in the house.

"Horace," he said, "find Lilian's songs for her," and turned away.

The girl gave a timid glance at him, and he looked back with a reassuring smile.

"Let us hear what you can do, my dear," he laughed. "None of your newfangled runs, but just an old simple song, such as I heard in my youth."

And Lilian sung him the old refrain, "Home Sweet Home."

There was a ring in her voice which reminded him of her mother's, and tears rose to his eyes as he listened, but Lilian's powers fell very far short of those of the dead woman.

She was nervous, moreover, and did not feel that she had done her best, and was in haste to quit her position.

"Dela, *do* sing us something!" she said eagerly.

"Yes, Adela, do!" added the Baronet. "I often hear you sing over your work—a soft little lullaby."

"Must *I* give you an old song too?" she queried kindly.

"By all means, yes; my ears are not educated to the new."

"Some of the ballads of the present day are really beautiful; I must teach you to like them, I think; but I will humour you to-night."

And she sat down, and gave that touching old song, "She wore a Wreath of Roses," and the salt tears fell one by one unheeded down the old man's wrinkled cheeks; for the wife he loved, who was growing to perfection in God's garden, used to sing that very song to him; and once more she seemed to be there with him in the old room, and all his guests were for the time being forgotten. She and he were alone, and their love was new.

He gave Adela no word of thanks, but sat as one spell-bound, and she sympathising in his mood, and understanding it, crept away into the dimly-lighted conservatory, as she thought unobserved; and leaning her aching head against the cold glass of the door, she looked out with blind eyes into the darkness beyond.

"It is like my life!" she murmured

passionately. "Black as Erebus! Oh! Cecil, Cecil! how you have made me suffer!"

"Dela! what is the matter?" asked Lilian's soft voice near her.

"Nothing Lil, nothing."

"Dela, darling, I heard what you said just now."

"Did you?" returned the other wearily. "Well, it did not amount to much."

"That is true; it only told me what I have long known, that you are unhappy, and I feel such a wretch to be in the sunshine while you are in the shadow."

"Nonsense, Lil. I do not pretend to be high-minded, and say I am *content* to be in the shadow. I should love the sunshine as well as any other girl; but, Lil, I do strive to *grow* in it, to do what good I can in my generation. I don't want it to wither me up, and render me useless; but it is very hard to do so."

"Poor, poor old girl! So it *is* Cecil, after all. You once promised to tell me all about it."

"Did I promise? Well, I couldn't, Lil, then, and I can't now. I may get used to it by-and-by, and be able to do so, but not yet. Don't ask me questions, there's a dear, only thank Heaven that you have gained the heart of a man who would as soon mistrust his own honour as your faith and love."

"Surely no one who knows you *could* mistrust you, Scamp, darling?"

"There! there! I have said enough! too much. Go away, Lil; I want to be alone."

"You would not be, if I obeyed you. Lord Carruthers has been waiting for you as faithful as a watch-dog. His eyes have been fixed upon the door ever since you passed in here."

"Oh! let me have a little peace to-night, there's a dear girl," said Adela impatiently.

"I wish you liked that man, Dela," whispered Lilian. "He is good and true."

"I can well believe it; but, oh! Lilian, to love once with me means to love to the end, and I shall love Cecil while life lasts."

"It may come right, darling," said Lilian, very softly. "Who ever could have dreamed that Horace and I should now be so happy?"

"Lil, my trouble makes me seem selfish, but I am more than glad and thankful for your joy."

"If *you* are selfish, Dela, darling, may all the world become so," ended Lilian with warmth, as she clasped her friend's hand lovingly in her own.

. . . .

The carriage was summoned, and the party broke up.

After warmly thanking Sir Richard for all his kindness to their son, and his hospitality to themselves, Mr Lake and his good-tempered wife withdrew to get into their outdoor-clothing, warm wraps having been necessitated by the fact that they had been driven to the Hall in an open trap. Mr and Mrs Thorndyke, who had come in the close carriage, lagged behind, to tell the Baronet how rejoiced they were at the issue events had come to.

"It is so much better sanctioned," remarked the Rector wisely. "Lilian was too staunch ever to have given her lover up. It was easy enough to tell her that it was her *duty* to be obedient; but who in their heart could blame the girl for her truth?"

"They say everything comes to the man who waits!" returned Sir Richard; "and so the young people have found it; and no one is much more surprised than I am myself," he laughed.

"I wish I could see Adela as happy as Lilian!" said Mrs Thorndyke wistfully, as she watched Lord Carruthers saying a few parting words to the girl.

"I am sure she could be if she chose!" replied Sir Richard meaningly, as his eyes followed hers.

"I quite agree with you!" said the Rector; "but girls are full of strange fancies! When we wish things they are dead against them, but if they once find out we consider a man a detrimental, it is all up with the affair. No one else will do!"

"There is no incentive like opposition," laughed the Baronet. "If I had another daughter, I should *insist* upon her marrying the man to whom I most strongly objected. With the light of experience thrown upon the subject, I should have no fears as to the result."

Horace and Lilian here came out from behind the heavy folds of the window curtains.

"I heard your treason, father!" she said, with a shy smile.

"Who was to know you were in there, star-gazing?" replied Sir Richard, somewhat taken aback. "You should have coughed to attract our attention! Listeners seldom hear any good of themselves!"

"Well, we did not much mind what we heard; did we, Horace?"

"Come, lad, we can make room for you in the carriage! It will save you the run home!" said the Rector kindly.

"I fear my legs are not telescopic!" returned Horace. "No, thanks, I shall enjoy the walk! Lilian and I have ascertained that it is a lovely night; and I want a word with Sir Richard before I start!"

"As you will. Where is Adela?"

She stepped forward readily.

"Good-night, my dear! You will come home for a few days before your departure—to get your things together?"

"I will come to enjoy a peep at you and mother!" she corrected.

"Well, it sounds prettier put like that?" and he stooped and kissed her.

"Suppose we look for you to-morrow, then?" suggested Mrs Thorndyke.

"With Sir Richard's permission," replied the girl, turning towards him.

"Say the next day, my dear! I shall be tired to-morrow, and dull too! Excitement brings reaction! Stay with me to-morrow, child!" he said softly.

"Very well! The following morning, then, expect me, mother dear!" and she raised her face for her mother's kiss.

Good-byes were exchanged, and the carriage went swiftly away down the drive, Lord Carruthers' pulling up at the Hall door in its stead.

"Then we shall meet again at Mentone?" said his lordship, as he took Adela's white hand within his own, and looked down into her eyes. "Miss Thorndyke, will you give me a welcome when I arrive?"

"We shall all do that!" she answered, in a matter-of-fact way; "and no doubt Sir Richard will be pleased to see one of his own countrymen again!" and she drew away her hand quietly, but firmly.

"You will find plenty of English families in Mentone!"

"Yes; but he has lived so quiet a life; he is not likely to know them."

"That is true."

"Is it pleasant there?"

"Very! Won't you enjoy sitting with open windows, even in winter time?"

"Immensely!"

"And you will revel in the spring flowers? They are simply exquisite."

"I am sure I shall. They are the fairest of all which the year produces, and that is saying something."

"Have you ever seen the conservatories at my home, Miss Thorndyke? You have never honoured Warminster Towers since I have been its owner, but you may have been there before then?"

"We have not much time for running about," replied Adela indifferently. "I don't think I ever was there, even in childhood."

"I should be so glad if the Rector and Mrs Thorndyke would bring you over to lunch one day. I should like you to see the hothouses, since you care for flowers."

"I am very fond of them, indeed, but you see my time at home will be brief. You must excuse my seeming ungracious, but we could not manage it."

He heaved a sigh of disappointment.

"I must hope for better luck upon your return," he said regretfully. "And now, good-bye. When next we meet it will not be upon English soil. Heaven bless you."

Then he turned from her, mingled with the rest, and went his way.

CHAPTER V.

"GOOD-BYE."

"WAIT for me, darling, to say good-night," whispered Horace to his *fiancée*. "I want a word with your father before I leave."

"I will be in the library," she answered promptly; and passing over to Adela, who was standing thoughtfully apart, she linked her hand through her arm, and led her from the room.

"Hallo!" said Sir Richard, watching the movement. "What's up now? They have left us alone on purpose."

"That is quite true, sir. I asked Lilian to let me have a word with you."

"I thought everything was settled," answered the Baronet, somewhat impatiently. "Are you not satisfied with the arrangements?"

"Sir Richard," said Horace gravely, "do you really wish me to go to Mentone with you?"

"Lilian does, and that is much the same thing," he answered. "Don't you care about the trip?"

"More than I can tell you."

"Then the matter is settled. What is there to talk about? We shall start on the morning of this day week."

"Sir Richard, you have been more than kind,—most thoughtful and generous in your offers to my father concerning me; but when he accepted them, conditionally upon my liking the scheme, he was not aware of the relations existing between us. He considered it a business transaction, for which you were ready and willing to pay handsomely. As it is, although I gladly accept your kind invitation to accompany you to Mentone, and stay with you there, you must allow me to decline, with many thanks, remuneration for services I do not perform; and my young brother will, I feel sure, do my work in the office during my absence."

"Does your father agree to this?" asked Sir Richard.

"Of course he does, sir."

"Did he suggest this line of conduct?" he inquired, with a keen look.

"Not exactly."

"Did *you*?"

"I told my father my opinions."

"And did he agree with them?"

"They came fresh to him; he had not considered the subject, but he sees that I am right."

The Baronet remained in thought.

"You're a proud lad," he said at length, with a smile breaking out over his handsome face. "Are you quite decided in this course?"

"Quite!"

"Well, well, I like you none the less for your independence. I suppose you will not refuse to accept bread and cheese in my house?"

"Certainly not, sir. I am more than grateful for the kind thought which will enable me to spend the next few months by my dear girl's side, and I thank you very much. I have had a very happy day, the happiest I have ever known, and now I must not keep you up."

"No, lad. Send Adela to me, and make your adieux to your ladye love," and he shook Horace warmly by the hand.

"Dela," said the latter, as he entered

the library, "we have *you* to thank for it all. Is there nothing we can do to prove our appreciation of your kindness? No brightness we can bring into *your* life?"

"Nothing, my friend," she answered, with a smile, "think of Lilian, not of me. Don't you know, Horace, I'm always bright?"

"Scamp, Scamp, don't tell tarradiddles!" said Lilian, winding her arms about her.

"Did not Sir Richard ask for me?" she questioned suddenly.

"Yes, he did," confessed Horace.

"Then why did you not tell me so?" she cried impatiently, and walked quickly towards the door; but before she reached it she turned back. "I'm a regular Goth," she said, with regret in her tone, "but I am more pleased than I can explain, at all that has happened to-day.

Dear old friends both, I congratulate you from my heart."

Then she kissed Lilian, held Horace's hand, and passed quietly out of the room.

"Is it Carruthers?" asked Horace, after a pause. "Dela cares for some one, I'm sure."

"No, it is not his lordship," replied Lilian sadly. "I wish she could like him, he would make her a loving husband, and he worships her."

"I have thought so for a long time. Well, who is it, Lilian?"

"Why *you*, of course, boy. Does not your vanity tell you so?"

"Can't say it does. Had Scamp made love to me, little woman, who knows but she might have *cut you out!*" he laughed.

"And saved me from a life of misery, eh? Well, dear, these things *are written*,

I suppose, and you and I were meant to torment each other, as you couldn't get Scamp."

"Do you think I ever tried, darling?" he asked, looking at her with a lover's eyes.

"I am quite sure of one thing," she returned roguishly.

"And that is?"

"That Dela never did, or you, or any other man, would have been at her feet," she continued, with a smile.

"Then why is she sad at heart, for that is what I feel she is?"

"Horace, our dear old Scamp doesn't tell her secrets, even to me, so it is of no use for you to question me about them."

"All right, pet, I understand; I'm not to know," he laughed.

"No, nor I either, for the matter of that, and it does not seem loyal to talk of, and speculate upon, what she doesn't wish to tell, does it?"

"Perhaps you're right, dear; and now, sweetheart, I must go. Are you *quite* contented with your choice, little woman?"

"Quite," she answered, letting both hands creep into his, while her soft dark eyes met his own, full of confidence and deep affection.

"I would not exchange you for the most eligible *parti* in the whole world."

Then he stooped and kissed her with a lover's fervour.

"I'm the happiest man on earth, darling," he whispered "*the* very happiest, my little love!"

"And *I'm* not altogether miserable, old boy," she answered mischievously, as she nestled in his arms in perfect confidence.

"That is good hearing," he laughed; "happiness is making you saucy, Lilian!"

"Papa wants me to be saucy, you know."

"Does he? Did he tell you so?"

"He wishes me to be like Dela, and she is saucy, goodness knows!"

"She is Scamp," replied her lover, "and you are my own dear love. Scamp is the dearest girl in all the world, and you are dearer still; but neither of you must be like the other, or both would be spoilt."

"I think I understand, Horace," said Lilian softly. "I must be myself to you because you have learnt to love me as I am. Papa is going to care for me, as he wants me to be, and the nearer I can come up to Dela the more he will like me, so I must be very bright and cheery with him."

"Right you are, little one; and now, good-night. Heaven bless you, dear! Only two years more, Lilian, and then—"

He clasped her to him in an almost boyish ecstasy.

"If you want me, then, don't choke me now," she gasped. "I call this ill-usage."

"You will have plenty of it, pet," he laughed. "You have given yourself to me, you know—have you not?"

"Horace, you must go," she said suddenly.

"Little traitor! you are laying up heavy punishment, to be paid in the future with interest."

"I'm not greatly afraid," she answered, laying her head against his shoulder, and turning her ripe lips up for his farewell kiss. "Is it not delightful that you are to go abroad with me, love?"

"It is indeed, Lilian, dear; your old father is a brick. We shall grow awfully fond of him, I am sure."

"I wish he had always been like this," said she, thoughtfully.

"I don't, or you would never have disobeyed him, and stuck to me."

"In that case, I don't either," she confessed, in a soft voice, "for you are the one being in the world I *could not do without*. Much as I love them both, I could *live without* papa and Dela; but, Horace, I could *not* without *you!*" and she clasped her arms about his neck, and clung to him.

"Lovey, I am so glad, so very, very glad!" he whispered back, and held her a willing captive in his strong embrace.

. . . .

"Adela," said Sir Richard, as she entered the room, "have I done all as you wished?"

"You have been most kind and noble, you dear old man," she answered, coming to his side, and passing her hand gently over his silver hair. "You have fought a brave battle, and come out a generous victor!"

"If I have done what is right, Adela, I have to thank you, and you only. I confess I have not gone through to-day without pain."

"And yet I have never seen you look happier."

"There is pleasure even in the sacrifice of self, child, when one knows that the holocaust is appreciated," he returned, with a smile.

"Unselfish pleasure is the purest of all," said Adela. "And now let me thank you for all you have done to please me, and to make Lilian happy," and she stooped and kissed him.

"I am more than repaid, my dear," he returned, and pressed his lips to her white hand, like any young gallant.

"And now," she continued, "you must

be very tired. Let me give you an arm upstairs, you will be glad of a long rest. Don't let any one call you to-morrow; have your sleep out, and ring the bell when you awake."

"I'll follow your advice, my dear. I confess I'm fairly done up."

And he leant heavily upon the girl's arm.

"You must save up all your strength for your journey," she added.

"Adela, I am so glad you are coming with us, my dear." he said earnestly. "My life will be a dull thing when you go out of it, my child. Do you think the Rector would let me adopt you?"

She looked round with an amused smile, but his face was very grave.

"Would not papa laugh if you asked him?" she replied merrily.

"You don't think he would consent?"

"You forget I am his one little ewe-lamb," she said gently.

"No, no! I do not, but he has his wife; he does not need you as I do," he answered, with feeling.

"Do you care for my company so very much?" she said kindly. "Well, I shall be by your side to tease you for a long, long time. You will be quite weary of me before the winter is out."

"Perhaps it would be better for me if I could be so," he replied sadly.

Adela smiled.

"It would not be flattering to my self-esteem," she admitted. "No, Sir Richard, don't let me stay till you grow tired of me."

"No fear of that, my child," he replied earnestly, looking at her beautiful changing face. "No one could do that."

And he left her at his chamber door with no other word of farewell.

The intervening week between Lilian's birthday and the day upon which the party were to start for Mentone, was a bustling one.

Adela had thoroughly enjoyed her little bit of home-life, greatly as she was petted and made much of at Marsden Hall. Her father's kind words, and her mother's gentle looks, were very sweet to her, after having been in a measure without them for some time; and the hours they spent together at their needlework, sitting at the Rector's side by the fire, were happy and peaceful ones.

"I wonder," said Mr Thorndyke upon one of these occasions, "I wonder I have not heard from Egerton. I wish he had chanced to come in upon us while you were at home, Adela — don't you?"

The girl's fingers trembled so that she could not for the moment make a single stitch; but in a short time she raised a quiet white face to her father's.

"I daresay he will get on very well without me, papa. I was scarcely more than a child when we struck up a friendship, and that was a very long while ago."

"Yes, but he has been here since that." Then, after a thoughtful pause, Mr Thorndyke added,—"I don't think you hit it off with Egerton so well during his last visit, my dear?"

A roseleaf hue crept into her pale cheeks, but she met her father's eyes bravely.

"Perhaps not," she replied, very quietly. "Twenty years' disparity makes people look at things from a different standpoint, of course."

"I thought so," laughed the Rector, "and neither you nor Cecil would give up your opinions to save your lives."

"*I* should not, decidedly, unless I saw myself to be in the wrong."

" Would you *then?* "

" Certainly. Would not *he?* "

"I hardly know; Cecil is rather what men call 'pig-headed'; no doubt he considers it firmness, but I don't; yet he has a generous nature, and if he could be *made* to see that he had been wrong or unjust, I think he would be more than willing to make reparation."

"But it would be hard to make him see his error?"

"Very, I should fancy."

"That is quite the estimate I have formed of his character."

"You have been studying it, then?"

"It is a way I have, dad," she answered, with a smile. "I cannot go through the world with my eyes shut. I must analyse my friends' peculiarities when I am in their company; and, do you know, I often find that they are so different from what we fancy them to be."

"Sir Richard, for instance."

"Yes, indeed. Who ever could have believed him to be what he is; shut away as he has been behind that screen of reserve, which he had placed around him."

"I have always known him for a good man, although of late, like all the world, I thought sorrow had hardened and soured him."

"He is not hard, dad, nor sour either, but he has suffered very much."

Then after a pause, Adela looked up with one of her own smiles.

"Do either of you want to get rid of me?" she asked.

"To get rid of you, child! Heaven forbid!" returned her mother, with a look of surprise.

"Don't be alarmed, mother mine; I'm not going to be married, or any thing dreadful," she laughed; "but Sir Richard would like to adopt me, *if you* are *tired* of me at home."

"Greedy old rascal!" exclaimed the Rector, joining in her mirth; "he has had you for weeks, and is going to have you for months, and now he wants to keep you altogether! No, no, my little Dela, your poor dad must not be quite forgotten."

Adela laid her work down, and knelt in her old childish way beside him.

"Do you *want* to go, my dear?" he asked, after a pause.

"No, father," she answered readily. "I am very fond of Sir Richard and Lilian, but fonder still of you and mother."

"I need not have inquired," he asserted, with a look of contentment. "Need I, my dear?"

"I don't think so, dad," she replied, and laid her head upon his shoulder, and was very quiet and still.

Time does not tarry; and Adela's trunks had to be packed for her journey. As she looked at them, and then at her parents, a pang of regret shot through her warm heart.

She did not at all like to leave them, now the hour for doing so was drawing near. She was really going for the sake of Sir Richard, whose mind appeared set upon the project, and she did not wish to disappoint him, because he was still weak and ill, and because he had done so much to please her.

But now that she looked at her father, the thought came to her that he was altering very much, and a fear took possession of her.

Words came to her lips. She longed to ask him if he were ill, but she wisely kept silence until he left the room, when she inquired anxiously about his health.

"I do not think he is really ill, darling," answered her mother kindly; "and you must not spoil your holiday by fretting about him; but we must not hide from ourselves the fact that your dear father is not strong. I made him see the doctor yesterday, and he says there is no cause for alarm if he will only take moderate care of himself."

"But when did he ever do that, mamma? Papa's energy is beyond his power."

"Quite true, dear girl. He says himself he means to *wear out*, and not to *rust out*."

"Yes, but for our sakes he must not wear out before his time," replied Adela, with a sad smile. "Shall I beg him not to work so hard, before I go?"

"Do, dear, if you like. I will leave you alone with him when he comes in."

He did so shortly after, and the girl placed her arms fondly about his neck.

"Father, dear," she said, "I have a parting favour to ask."

"Have you, my child? If it be in my power, it is granted before you name it."

"It is quite within your power, dad. I want you to take more care of yourself,—not to go out all weathers, and to work less hard altogether."

"You have asked what is difficult, Dela. I cannot refuse to bury a man because it is raining, nor to marry a couple when I am tired; but I will remember your affectionate solicitude, and spare myself when it is possible; and with that my little girl must be satisfied. Come back with roses upon your cheeks instead of lilies, my darling, and I shall be repaid for having deprived myself of your company."

"And let me see you look hale and strong when I return, dear dad, and then, please Heaven, we shall have a bright spring and a happy summer together."

He kissed her, spoke to her of her

journey, and then she went upstairs to dress. Every little detail of her pretty chamber seemed dear to her now she was about to leave it. Things which she had scarcely before noticed, suddenly obtruded themselves upon her attention. Her father's books, her mother's work, all speaking to her of a happy home-life.

A wave of regret flooded her mind. How little she had thought of that home-life lately!

Her heart had been so filled with painful longings, and useless thoughts of the past, that the happiness which really was her own, had been dwarfed out of its truly beautiful proportions.

She had not realised it while she had her home, but now that she was leaving it, even for a time, the truth became apparent. Her eyes were opened.

She groped her way downstairs, almost

blinded with tears; was clasped in her father's arms, and held to her mother's breast. She heard their loving voices, wishing her "Godspeed" in a far-off dreamy way, and was soon in the Hall carriage, going towards Marsden as quickly as the horses could carry her.

"It is hard to part with her," said the Rector, as it passed out of sight, "but I could not refuse Sir Richard's request. We must never forget that we are indebted to him for this living, which enabled us to marry. Dearly as I loved you, Mary, I could never have asked you to be a curate's wife on a hundred and fifty pounds a year."

"I would have accepted you, Edward, if you had only had the fifty without the hundred," she returned, with a loving smile.

"I believe it," he said earnestly. "My dear, you have been a good and faithful wife to me, and the knowledge that such is the case, and that you have cheered me along life's road for many years, and often through rugged paths, will give you contentment when the snows of time have fallen upon your head, and you may, perchance, no longer have me by your side," and he drew his wife's hand through his arm and led her indoors.

CHAPTER VI.

SEEN THROUGH A LEAFY SCREEN.

ENTONE proved all which Adela and her friends could desire.

The damp and fog-born coughs soon ceased, bronchitis was laid aside, roses bloomed upon the girl's cheeks, and the hue of health was seen upon those of Sir Richard; while Horace, between happiness, and change, and rest, looked more "fit" than he had ever done before.

Sir Richard was beginning to like his society, and to seek it, and although he was not willing to acknowledge it, even to himself, he no longer felt any regret at his daughter's choice.

Almost every day the old Baronet might be seen leaning upon the young man's arm, with a bright and interested face; listening to his news, and his amusing conversation.

Some materials strike sparks out of the dullest metals.

It was so with Horace.

He had always something to say, and whatever the theme, he managed it so as to make it worth talking about; and Adela and Lilian looked on, well content.

Among the English people at Mentone that season were Lord Lynestone and his young wife and little son; and Cecil Egerton, at the earnest request of the former, went thither to confer with him about the boy's future.

Lord Lynestone was sinking slowly. He had no especial disease to which medical science could be of avail. It was with him a general decadence, a failing of nature.

He was considerably above the age of man, and knew that he could expect nothing else; and he was prepared for the end. Nay, he would have welcomed it, weary with the journey of life, but for the sake of the two he must leave unshielded in the world. Still he trusted to his nephew to stand by them, and aid them when he should have paid nature's last debt.

He felt that his marriage had been very hard upon Cecil, and he now meant to leave him such a fortune as would render him independent of the service, whenever he desired to retire from it, after his many years of soldiering. It seemed as though the old Earl could not die until he had commended his wife and child to his care.

Lord Lynestone's had been a somewhat romantic marriage.

He had for twenty years had a private secretary, who had lived in his house, and attended to all his affairs; one Captain D'Arcy, who passed among them as a single man, and was believed to be such by the Earl himself, until the date of the Captain's sudden illness and unexpected death.

Then he sent for his patron, and, in great distress of mind, told him a sad history.

Captain D'Arcy had married in his youth a lady of good family and expectations, but the marriage had been a clandestine one.

Had it proved happy, the young man would have soon acknowledged it to the world, but the tempers of the two were unsuited, and they speedily agreed mutually each to go their own way, and leave the other untrammelled; he plunging into a vortex of dissipation, which soon obliged him to leave his regiment, and she to return to live in her father's house of ease and luxury, which she bitterly regretted having ever left.

Once only had he seen her after that, when their little girl was born.

Then she had sent for him to see the child, and he had gone.

He found her in a London lodging, she being supposed to be abroad with some friends, who, knowing of her secret marriage, were willing to keep her counsel.

He called again at a later date, and found both mother and child gone, and the former had left no address. He applied to the post-office, but none had been lodged there either, and he returned to his club in a state of disgust, determining to trouble himself no more about a woman who cared so little for him.

Neither she nor the child could want, he knew, for although she would not be able to take her little one home to her father's, without acknowledging her marriage, her pin-money alone amounted to a large sum, out of which she could well afford to pay for the keep of her infant.

Shortly after, through an influential friend, Captain D'Arcy obtained the position in Lord Lynestone's household, which he retained until his death.

During his last hours the past troubled him, and he charged Lord Lynestone to let his wife know of his decease, receiving from him a promise to see both her and his daughter.

His lordship therefore went straight to her father's mansion in Bankshire, there to learn a sad story.

He had been ruined ten years before, by

a bank failure, and the family had split up, each to earn their own living as best they could.

He had considerable difficulty in finding Mrs D'Arcy, but he had made a promise to a man now dead, and he was determined to fulfil it, if possible.

When he did find her, it was in a state of almost poverty; her daughter was with her, her constant nurse and companion.

Mrs D'Arcy had been no mean artist as an amateur, and she had supported herself and her child, at first with but small difficulty.

But the long hours of labour, the loss of brightness in her life, the poorer fare, the confinement, soon told upon her health.

She was too proud to apply to her husband to help her, by whom she had not stood in her younger days, nor had she his address, save that of the club to which she had directed in days gone by.

She did not know of his long residence at Lynestone, as the Earl's secretary.

She and Rosamond occupied two small rooms in a pretty cottage at Richmond, and the girl now went to London with her mother's paintings, which grew fewer and fewer as her strength gradually diminished.

When Lord Lynestone arrived at Jasmine Cottage he was over fatigued, and his sad revelation made, the invalid had to bestir herself to wait upon him, for Rosamond was out.

When the girl returned, she thought the old man so ill that she went for a doctor, who said he must be put to bed at once, and carefully watched, for he was threatened with apoplexy.

Here was a terrible position for the D'Arcys. Rosamond carried their trouble to their kind landlady, who offered to give up her own airy bedroom to his lordship, and to help the girl to wait upon him; and there Lord Lynestone had to remain for a week, his household in a state of dismay at his unusual absence.

No apoplexy intervened; it was staved off by the doctor's careful treatment, and the old man went home.

But he could not forget Mrs D'Arcy and her beautiful young daughter, and before a month had elapsed, he wrote a formal proposal for fair Rosamond's hand, at the same time offering her mother a home at Lynestone. He had taken a fancy to the bright-faced girl, and thought this would be the best way to help them.

His offer was at once gladly accepted.

Love was a sealed book to Rosamond D'Arcy. She had had to toil early and late, and it seemed to her that a life of ease and pleasure would be Paradise.

The price she had to pay for it appeared nothing until her wedding-day; then her heart spoke—her womanhood cried out. She shrank from the future before her, and burning tears ran down her pale cheeks, for she knew that she was selling herself for this world's goods —knew that she had no love for the old man whom she must henceforth call husband.

But she drove back these natural feelings, and became Lady Lynestone, and she and her mother settled down in comfort in the beautiful home which was to have been Cecil Egerton's.

There was to be no more toil now, no more drudgery, no more poverty, but the change had come too late for Mrs D'Arcy. She lived to see Lord and Lady Lynestone's little boy, and then faded away, being united to the husband in death, with whom she had elected not to remain in life.

Rosamond had made the old man a good and patient wife and nurse.

He was too infirm to take her out into the world, as she had hoped and dreamed, and well it was for her that such was the case.

With her dazzling beauty and youth, it was scarcely likely that her warm young heart would not have claimed some other kindred one for its own; and in a mind like hers the struggle between love and duty would have been a fearful ordeal for the young wife to pass through.

In her quiet and beautiful home, with her bonnie boy to interest and amuse her, she was at peace, and content; not pining for pleasure which she had never known. And there she remained for three more years, when the doctors ordered his lordship to a warmer climate.

They travelled from place to place, but even the air of Italy and Switzerland cannot rejuvenate, and the man of medicine knew that the beginning of the end had begun.

Lord Lynestone wished to die in his ancestral halls, but the homeward journey was pronounced to be too much for him; but his desire grew even more urgent, and it was decided that his removal should be attempted as soon as his nephew arrived, and he reached Mentone upon the same day as Sir Richard Freemantle and his party; whereas Lord Carruthers, who had travelled more quickly, had been already a couple of days on the spot, and had been devoting his time to making various arrangements for the comfort and pleasure of his friends from Marsden Hall.

Among other things, he determined to

procure some flowers to get placed in Adela's and Lilian's rooms, which he felt he could easily manage through the servants.

When at the florist's, he was strangely struck by the beauty of a lady who was choosing the fairest blossoms she could obtain, which he heard her say were for an invalid.

When she went away he inquired who the beautiful girl was, and learnt that this was Lord Lynestone's young wife, so soon, as all the world knew, to become a widow; and a great pity for her filled his mind. He seemed obliged to think of her, compelled to it by the force of her great beauty.

And he found himself asking, again and again, whether by any possibility this fair young creature *could* love the infirm old man with whom she was mated? and his own heart answered "No" emphatically.

Lord Carruthers' flowers were duly admired by Adela and Lilian upon their arrival, but one was as innocent as the other as to whose kindness they were indebted for them.

They found by the local paper, in the visitors' list, that he had arrived before them, and he left his card upon the first evening, with his address, and made inquiries for them after their journey; but delicacy prevented his breaking in upon their privacy so soon.

When Cecil Egerton reached the beautiful villa in which his uncle had taken up his abode, he saw at once the desire to go home had come upon him too late. He had a long and earnest talk with the dying man, who retained his faculties clear to the end.

He heard from his own lips the whole history of his marriage, and understood the significance of the fact that the young widow, countess though she was, had scarcely a friend in the world; and his uncle pointed out to Cecil what a prize she would be, with her beauty and wealth, and how many adventurers would be about her path, to whom she might fall an easy prey, from her innocence and ignorance of the ways of the world.

And Cecil promised to do the best he could to shield and advise her; also undertaking the guardianship of the little lordling, and Lord Lynestone lay very quiet with his feeble hand in the strong one of his nephew.

"Rosamond," he said, as she entered the room, "it is too late!"

"What is too late, dear?" she asked sorrowfully, kneeling by his side, and looking tenderly into his drawn face.

"Too late to return home. But you will bury me there, Cecil? My bones would not rest in a strange place."

"I will respect your wishes in all ways, my dear uncle," he replied kindly.

"Rosamond," continued Lord Lynestone, "when I am gone you must look to Cecil for advice and guidance. If you are in any difficulty, my child, appeal to him. He will help you, for my sake!"

"I shall not forget," she answered softly.

"She has been a gentle wife, Cecil; and remember, I am not selfish enough to wish her to spend her life alone. She is young, and will, I hope, some day marry suitably. But, Rosamond, if you have any doubt as to the fitness of your choice, consult Cecil, and recollect that he was your husband's only relation."

Tears filled the sweet blue eyes, and words rose to her lips, springing from a tender heart.

She was trying to tell her dying lord

that no other should take his place, but he stopped her.

"Hush! my darling! I will listen to no such promises. I will not permit you to make them. Who knows what the future may hold for you? Remember I *wish* you to be happy! Now, kiss me, child, and let me sleep."

She obeyed him, and she and Cecil sat there watching, listening to the laboured breathing.

The doctor came, but did not disturb him. He called Cecil on one side, and told him he would probably pass away in his sleep, and he was right.

Cecil went over to the young widow, and taking her hand, tried to lead her from the room.

"Let me stay," she pleaded. "I cannot leave him!"

"My dear," he answered gently. "The end was indeed peaceful. *He has left you!*"

"No, no," she answered, in an awed voice. "He cannot be dead!"

She leant over him.

He breathed no more.

Then she stooped and kissed him, weeping the while, and let Cecil take her from the chamber.

. . . .

That evening Cecil went out upon various matters in connection with his uncle's death, and to make arrangements for the conveyance of his body to England; and as he stood within one of the shops, he heard a voice which made his heart stand still, and saw a tall slight figure pass in company with another girl.

Sir Richard and Horace were in front of them, but he did not perceive them. His whole attention was taken up by Adela and Lilian, both of whom he recognised.

The former was looking bright and happy, as well as the latter, for they were expressing their satisfaction at the good terms which had begun to exist between Sir Richard and Horace.

Had Adela turned round, she would have seen her lover watching her. As it was, the carriage was awaiting them at the end of the next street, and as soon as they reached the corner they got in and drove off. So when Cecil made up his mind to follow them, they were no longer visible, nor could he understand what had become of them.

Suddenly he looked up, and saw the publishing shop, where the list of visitors was printed; but upon application for one, he found it would not be out till the following morning.

But the transfer of a heavy coin from Cecil's pocket to that of the salesman, brought the offer of the names and addresses of any of the new arrivals he might wish to know about, and he left the office with the information that Miss Thorndyke was staying at Greenholme with Sir Richard Freemantle and his family; and that night Adela's *espiègle* face chased away the sweet, sad one of Lady Lynestone, and even that of the dead Earl himself, and by morning Cecil had made up his mind to call and see Adela,—see for himself whether he was forgotten, or if the light of love would ever again shine from her beautiful eyes for him.

He had been wildly, madly jealous. Reason was crushed out of his mind by the stronger feeling.

Every mail he had expected to hear that the woman he loved was betrothed to another, and that other was Lord Carruthers; but no such news reached him.

The last he had heard of her, was that she had gone to Marsden Hall to help Lilian to nurse her father, so he was not greatly surprised to find her, even at Mentone, in their company.

He still loved her with every pulse of his exacting heart. She was just as needful to his happiness as ever.

If he could once see her, he should soon know whether she had shut him out from her love.

One moment he told himself it was no wonder if she had done so, for she was a proud girl, and he had left her with scarce a word.

The next he fiercely repeated that there was no other course open to him, as he had assured himself at Winsthorpe, and over and over again since that sad day when her self-will and his mistrust had wrecked their joint happiness.

Sleep would not come to him. Restlessly he paced his chamber, impatient for the morning, that he might present himself at Greenholme; and before noon he stood with his hand upon the latch of the gate, with a wildly-beating heart.

The path up to the house by which he entered the grounds was not the carriage drive, but wound among beautiful shrubs and ferns, being almost at times hidden from view.

As he followed it, going towards the house, Adela's voice came to him, and he stopped with a sudden longing to see her unseen, and peered through the leafy screen.

She was sitting under the verandah, and advancing in her direction across the lawn was a tall, fair young man.

Cecil Egerton's heart stood still. The blood then surged with a mad rush through his veins.

He clenched his powerful right hand,

and dug his heel savagely into the gravel path.

"Dela," said the fair man, "which will you have—red or white?"

"Oh, white for me!" she answered, with a bright smile, looking up at him.

> "'Roses red and roses white,
> As if pale with love's despair,
> As if pale with love's despair,'"

he sang, as he handed it to her.

"A great deal *you* know of love's despair, you old rascal!" she laughed.

"I *should* have known it, Scamp, but for you," he returned earnestly. "You have been my good angel."

"A wingless one, I fear," she retorted. "And now see—I have no pin."

"But *I have*. You perceive that I'm not an engaged man for nothing; every lover should be made to carry pins for his lady's needs. Here you are, Dela, or better still, let me put it on for you.

I'm getting quite an expert at that sort of thing already."

Adela rose from her chair, and willingly allowed Horace to pin on the roses he had given her.

There was no reserve, no shyness between these two; there was not the least consciousness, nor the faintest fear of their misunderstanding each other.

But Major Egerton misunderstood them. The old jealousy was raging in his breast.

"That man again — curse him!" he muttered, through his clenched teeth. " Let her have him — he is a better match than I shall ever be!" he added bitterly, "and she knows it," and he turned away with uneven steps, going out again by the gate he had entered with so light a heart, heavy enough now —heavy as lead.

It was agony to him to see her accept love gifts from another, to watch him pin them upon her shoulder with a lover's freedom, to hear him say she had saved him from despair, to listen to his opinion as to his own improvement as her lady's-maid, since his engagement to her.

Every word entered his very soul, and quivered there like a barbed and poisoned arrow.

He had told himself from month to month that it was all over between them, but never with such dead certainty as now.

She was engaged to another. Horace's own words had been the funeral knell of all his hopes.

He looked ten years older when he once more entered the villa of his dead uncle. Lady Lynestone gazed at him in wonder, questioned him as to whether he was ill; but Cecil was not the man to appreciate the prettiest woman's sympathy, if she were not the one woman in the world for him.

So he forced himself to talk to her of the funeral arrangements, earnestly persuading her to remain at Mentone with her boy, while he went to England with his sad charge, and saw his uncle laid to rest among his ancestors.

"If you say it is right, Cecil, it must be so," she answered, "for my dear lord bade me trust you."

So Cecil asked a few people whom he knew to be kind to the gentle young widow until his return, and set out upon his melancholy journey.

His path and Adela's had again met and diverged, and she little guessed how near she had been to having her lover at her feet once more.

CHAPTER VII.

"I COULD NOT GIVE YOU LOVE FOR LOVE."

AS Cecil Egerton listlessly ran his eye over the list of visitors at Mentone, he was not in the least surprised to see the name of Lord Carruthers among them, and he crushed the paper with an impatient hand, and flung it aside.

At one moment he decided to go to Winsthorpe, and upbraid his old friend the Rector for not letting him know the truth about Adela.

The next he saw the absurdity of such a step.

He had never, by word or look, taken Mr Thorndyke into his confidence, and how could he expect it in return from him, or sympathy either?

On the contrary, the Rector would be rejoicing in the engagement, which, to him meant lifelong loneliness; for well he knew that Adela's place in his heart could never be taken by another.

Perhaps his old friend had even laid pressure upon his child, to persuade her to accept this good match, which he had himself so ardently desired.

Not that Adela could have needed much persuasion, he thought bitterly. She had seemed perfectly at home with the handsome young fellow who was familiarly fastening roses upon her dress.

Well! there was little wonder. He was

in youth's pride and prime; he was rich, and affluent; while *he*, Cecil Egerton, was but a soldier of fortune, a major in a marching regiment, with his best years already passed.

The train whirled him along through France, his mind excited and sad.

Would Adela have married him if he had now been Lord Lynestone?

He asked himself the question again and again, one moment, loyal in his rejection of the thought that riches or station would have altered her conduct one jot or tittle; the next, recklessly believing this, or any other evil of her.

England was reached at last.

It was not two years since he had visited Lynestone—his uncle's guest.

Now, he was accompanying all that remained on earth of the Earl back to the home he had loved.

He had lived honoured and respected,

and had died at a good old age, respected still, leaving a wife to mourn his loss—at any rate, for a little space—and a hostage to fortune in the shape of his merry, blue-eyed boy—now Lord Lynestone.

And Cecil, his acknowledged heir for so many years, was *not* to reign in the old place in his stead.

There was a large gathering to pay the last tribute to the dead man.

No plumes or black draperies were to be seen at the Earl's funeral. No black hearse, or mourning coaches.

But there was a procession of well appointed private carriages following the catafalque, which reached from the mansion to the chapel in the park, which although in reality a private one, was thrown open on Sundays for the people of Lynestone to worship in.

There the family vault was.

In the middle of the chancel stood a

rarely beautiful monument, upon which the gold-hued glass windows threw a seeming glory.

Four angels carved in white marble were guarding it, one at either corner, and the names of the Lynestones, from the days of the Saxon kings, were graven upon it.

Facing the altar was a door by which descent was made to the spacious vault below, in which those of this ancient family rested, who had died at home in peace, while the bones of many had bleached upon battlefields, and some had known only a watery grave.

Among his ancestors they laid the departed Earl, his coffin laden with white blossoms, and turned each man to his own home, save those who were invited to be present at the reading of the will.

There were the usual legacies to old

family retainers, and instructions as to various favourite horses.

Cecil Egerton was to receive twenty thousand pounds, as a mark of his uncle's affection, and was appointed his boy's sole guardian from the age of twelve to eighteen, when he was to be permitted to judge for himself of his future; but was recommended still to act under his guardian's advice.

To Rosamond, his Countess, the Earl left the sum of fifty thousand pounds absolutely; which she was to retain in the event of her marrying again.

She was to live at Lynestone, if she desired it, should she remain a widow, until her son married, upon which event taking place, she was to inhabit the Dower House upon the borderland of the Park.

The rents, etc., were to be allowed to accumulate as much as possible during the young Earl's minority, and the Countess was lovingly entreated to confer with Cecil Egerton, the Earl's loved and respected nephew, upon all matters of importance.

All that he *could* leave to his wife and to Cecil he had done. The rest was entailed property.

When all had been arranged at Lynestone, Major Egerton hesitated.

Should he fulful his half-made promise to go to Winsthorpe or no? and he decided in the negative.

He felt he could not bear to hear his old friends there speak of the coming wedding of the girl he loved so dearly.

So a few lines informed Mr Thorndyke that press of business would prevent his paying them his talked-of visit, as he must return to Mentone to arrange matters for his young widowed aunt; but he purposely omitted to mention his address there, as he did not wish the Rector to write to him.

The consequence was *he* immediately penned a line to Adela, and told her that Cecil Egerton would be in Mentone almost as soon as his letter could reach her.

Knowing nothing of his last fatal mistake, the girl let hope once more grow in her heart.

If he should return, and ask her again for an explanation of what he had been unable to understand, or she then to tell him, how gladly would she reveal what had at that time been her friend's secret.

Now, Cecil and all the world might know who her fair and handsome gentleman visitor had been, and why she had met him as she had done.

The love-letter would be explained; the bogie of Lord Carruthers being her lover would be blown to the four winds, and she—

Might she not be Cecil Egerton's once more? Would he not ask her again to be his wife? Would he not open his arms for her to nestle upon his breast? and should she not hear his heart beat true to her?

She was alone in her chamber thinking, and she held out her hands with a glad cry, as though he were there to clasp them.

She felt that he was coming, that he was not a great way off! If once they met, all would be explained.

She never even asked herself whether he loved her still. It never struck her to doubt his loyalty. She believed him to be as incapable of changing as herself.

A misunderstanding had parted them, not want of love.

She had almost forgotten his lack of trust, in her visions of reconciliation. She was restless, and changeful in her moods. Even Horace and Lilian could not make her out. Gay as a skylark one moment, the next wrapped in thoughtful reflection, singing a snatch of a song, playing some bars of a piece, and suddenly stopping; her book lying idle upon her lap, or read by jerks. She seemed always to be listening; listening for Cecil.

But days passed slowly by, and he never came.

Sir Richard was once more himself again, and he and Adela took daily walks together, while Horace and Lilian wandered in the country, side by side, avoiding the haunts of men; too happy in each other's company to desire further companionship. Sir Richard, on the contrary, liked to look about, and see the people, and the shops, so he and Adela went often to the more frequented parts.

About a week after she had heard from

her father that Cecil was at Mentone, she saw him, and he saw her.

He was in Lady Lynestone's open carriage, sitting by her side, with the little lord upon his knee.

His eyes met hers coldly, and he merely raised his hat as the carriage dashed past with its fast-stepping bays.

"Who is that, my dear?" queried the Baronet, looking after the retreating vehicle.

For the moment she was speechless, all the blood seemed to have congealed in her veins. She had seen her lover again. Her soul had gone out to him, and he had passed her with cold courtesy.

She heard her old friend's question in a dazed way. Then she knew that he had repeated it. The earth seemed to have retreated beneath her feet.

She felt faint and ill, but she aroused herself with an effort.

Her strong will once more asserted itself, and she answered, in a firm voice,—

"Major Egerton; you know he is an old friend of papa's."

"To be sure, though I have never seen him before, but he recognised you, my dear, and he will be certain to look you up. When he comes, Adela, make him understand that your father's friends are mine, and that he will be welcome at my house. He must come and dine with us."

"You are very kind," she answered simply, for she knew not what to say.

Her vision had been blown away by one glance from Cecil's cold eyes.

There was not even surprise in them. She saw that he knew perfectly that she was in the place, and he had laid down his line of conduct towards her beforehand.

He knew that she was there, and he had not sought her.

"And who was the lady, my dear?" continued the Baronet. "She was a very pretty woman, and young to be a widow."

"Yes, she was really beautiful," said Adela freely. "I think she must be Lady Lynestone, his uncle's widow. You will remember that when Lord Carruthers dined with us a day or two ago he was speaking of her as one of the sweetest-looking women he had ever seen."

"Ah! I recollect now, and she deserved his praise. Widows are fascinating little creatures, and Carruthers had better take care of his heart," and Sir Richard looked searchingly in her face.

"It is early days to be finding her a new husband," she said, somewhat reproachfully, "even though hers was believed to be only a *mariage de convenance;* but if she is as sweet as she looks, when a right time has elapsed, Lord

Carruthers might do far worse than become her second husband."

"And would none of his fair friends grieve at his desertion?"

She shrugged her shoulders.

"Who can tell? One thing I do know, *I* should not be one of them."

He remained in thought, then spoke suddenly,—

"*A mariage de convenance* was it? Yes, yes, I suppose so. There must be some strong motive to induce summer to waste its bright days upon winter. It was not likely she loved him, was it, Adela?"

"You have asked me a question I cannot answer; I never saw the late Earl."

"But, generally speaking, such love would not be likely, or possible?"

"Not likely, but certainly possible."

"You think so, my dear?" he said, looking at her with interest.

"It would not be like the love of two young hearts, perhaps; but I think a girl might be very fond of an old man, if he were what he ought to be, ripened in goodness with his years."

"There are not many such, my child. Ah! here comes Carruthers."

Then he turned to his lordship.

"We have just seen your widow," he laughed, "and a lovely little woman she is; but there was a good-looking fellow already in possession."

"Indeed! so soon? Who, may I ask?"

"Major Egerton; he's a friend of Miss Thorndyke's."

"Egerton! Why, she's his aunt!"

"His aunt! she does not look like it."

"I *should* have said his uncle's widow. His marriage must have been a great disappointment to Major Egerton, for he didn't marry till he was seventy-five or six."

"Ten years my senior!" cried Sir Richard, "and married to a pretty young girl. Well! there is a chance for me yet—eh, Carruthers?"

"I shouldn't like you for a rival if you entered the lists with me," laughed Lord Carruthers, and then he added mischievously, "perhaps Lady Lynestone would like another matured man, Sir Richard. Who knows?"

"Who indeed!" chuckled the Baronet; "but, to tell the truth, I looked upon *you* as her admirer, and was saying so to Miss Thorndyke as you came along."

Lord Carruthers coloured.

Although he had been thinking a good deal of the widow and her beauty, his affections were still Adela's, and it was far from pleasant for him to have such a suggestion made to her; and he longed for an opportunity to convince her that Lady Lynestone was nothing to him.

"You are very thoughtful, Sir Richard," he said, in a nettled voice, "but rather precipitate, as I have not even yet been introduced to the lady in question."

The Baronet laughed.

He knew exactly what his lordship felt. He had in fact laid the trap for him, for he had not yet quite put aside *his* idea of making Adela happy.

Lord Carruthers accompanied them home, and was invited by the Baronet to remain to dinner, so he sauntered to his hotel and dressed, and returned in plenty of time for that meal.

It was a beautiful evening, and the stars were shining overhead as bright as diamonds in the sky; and all but Sir Richard were tempted out into the garden.

"Go out, my dear," he said kindly to Adela. "I have not seen you look so pale since you left England. You are as white as the privet flower."

"If I am as hardy I shall not hurt," answered Adela, with a sad smile.

"My dear, is anything the matter?" he asked anxiously, looking at her heavy eyes.

"My head aches," she replied. "It is not much to talk about, is it?"

"The air will do it good, Adela; stay as long as you feel inclined. I shall take a nap most likely."

So she joined the other three, and they wandered about the grounds; she and Lord Carruthers in front. Suddenly she stopped, for Horace and Lilian were nowhere to be seen.

His lordship had no mind to miss the opportunity which had been made for him, either by design or accident, and turned to her, the moonlight falling upon his refined, well-cut features.

"Adela," he said softly, "I was most terribly vexed at what Sir Richard said to me to-day regarding Lady Lynestone."

"Yes, it is a mistake to make such speeches," she replied readily, "especially when they are made in reference to a recent widow. She would naturally be bitterly annoyed if she by chance heard of them; but of one thing you may rest assured, it was said thoughtlessly, and with no intention to give offence."

"All you say is quite right, Miss Thorndyke," he continued; "but you do not seem to understand the chief cause of my annoyance. I shame to say it was not delicacy for her ladyship's feelings."

"No?" she said interrogatively.

"No; it was the fear you should believe that I could think of, or wish, any other woman for my wife except yourself, Adela," he went on earnestly. "I have loved you now more than three years. No other woman has been aught to me during that time. Your image has filled my heart to overflowing. I have loved you, and I love you still, with a deep and earnest affection. Adela! Adela! my dear girl, have you no kind thought for me? Do you continue indifferent as to my happiness?"

"Lord Carruthers, I am not indifferent to your happiness at all," she answered kindly; "and, indeed, nothing could give me more pleasure than to hear that you were thoroughly content with your life."

"Then, dear one, let me hope that you will give a different answer to my prayer from that I received at Winsthorpe. I cannot be happy without you."

"You would not be so with me," she answered sadly.

"Should I not?" he replied, in a low, passionate voice, drawing her to him. "Adela, give me a trial; see if my deep devotion cannot satisfy you? Oh! my love, you do not dream what you are to me."

"Perhaps not," she answered. "And yet I think I do understand."

"You cannot, or you would not torture me by your coldness!" he cried.

"I am not cold," she said gently. "Indeed, I wish to be your friend; so much do I wish to be your friend that I will not shrink from giving myself cruel pain to prove it to you. Lord Carruthers, you will promise that what I say shall be sacred to you?"

"As sacred as my mother's honour," he replied solemnly.

"I am satisfied," she said, half under her breath. Then she turned and placed her cold hand in his.

"Would you wish a wife to lie in your bosom with a heart wildly longing for another man's love? Would you wish her to evade your kiss, because it is not his? To shrink from your tender words because they do not fall from his lips? To know that every fibre of her nature quivers at his touch, trembles at his footfall? To realise that whatever worship you give her, she loves *him* more? That all your deep affection can give her no joy, no happiness; her happiness being centred in another? Would such a wife make your comfort, my friend? Would you desire such a one for your life companion?"

"Heaven forbid!" he replied earnestly.

"Then never again think of me as aught but a friend. I like you truly; my love is beyond your reach!"

"Adela, can this be true?" he queried, in a pained voice, "or are you trying to cure me of my love? Are you building up this barrier to drive me away? Nothing but the knowledge that you belong to another will silence me, rest assured."

"My heart is not mine to give," she said sadly. "I might almost say 'I wish it were,' for your constancy touches me, and I believe you will be very good to the girl you marry; but I value your peace too much to accept your offer, knowing that I could not give you love for love,—could not satisfy your large heart. Dear Lord Carruthers, seek some gentle woman who would make you a loving, yielding wife and companion through life. I could not so wrong you as to take advantage of your devotion!"

"Adela," said his lordship, with feeling, "you have been very good to me; I know that it has cost you dearly to tell me the truth, for I fear your choice has not been a happy one?"

"No, it has brought me much sorrow," she confessed, with trembling lips.

"Will you make me one promise, dear?" he asked.

"Yes; I can trust you."

"If ever you overcome this fancy, and feel you are free to love another, and capable of wifely affection, you will let me know."

"Do not think of it; it is not a fancy, it is the love of years!"

"Adela, it is impossible that you can love in vain, if your lover is worthy of the name of man."

"He *is* worthy, believe me. I have no need to be ashamed of him," she said warmly, "he is brave and true!"

"Do not ask me to suppose the fault is yours, Adela; I cannot do it."

"Believe that there was no fault at all,

—that circumstances placed me in a false light!"

"And he could not trust you! My dear, I would have stood by you against all the evidence the combined world could produce. Adela, I would to Heaven your passion for this other were not so great, that I might shelter you from sorrow and care; but, my dear, I could not bear it. Every time I saw a cloud upon your white brow, I should feel that you were longing for *him*, and not for me. My soul would be torn with anguish," he added brokenly.

"I know it," replied she tenderly; "it would be so with every true man. My friend, you must *live it down!*"

"Yes! I must try and live it down, for the present I think I had better go away, and see whether your dear face will haunt me less elsewhere."

"You are quite right, Lord Carruthers,

and when it is done, come back. Let the past, with its dead hopes, never be spoken of between us, and let us be fast friends."

"That is a compact," he answered kindly. "And now, Adela, good-night; I cannot go back among the others. They must have guessed my secret; no doubt they will understand."

"Good-night," she said softly, "and believe that I am sorry to have given you pain!"

They clasped hands then warmly and firmly, and the night breeze seemed to take up her words, and to echo his sigh, as he parted from her, and went out into his life alone.

CHAPTER VIII.

A LAST LOOK AT THE ROSY WEST.

THE winter passed happily enough for all the *dramatis personæ* in our little life-drama.

To Horace and Lilian it brought unalloyed joy, to Sir Richard Freemantle peace and contentment; while Adela strove to enjoy the good things left to her, and to shut out from her mind that ever painful theme, Cecil Egerton, and her love for him.

It was not an easy task.

Nay, it was an impossible one, but she

hid her sufferings even from her dearest friends, and they thought her happy.

It was only when she was alone that her heart-weariness would at times overcome her, and break down the proud spirit which so bravely enabled her to hide her sorrow from an unsympathetic world, and sympathetic friends alike.

Lord Carruthers had been travelling from place to place and visiting among his kinsfolk and acquaintance, and everywhere the man whom Adela had rejected was a welcome guest and favourite.

To say he had ceased to care for her would be erroneous, but he thought of her now with no hope,—as a being beyond his reach.

He no longer intermingled her life with his, in imagination, and was one step upon the road to a more healthy state of mind.

Bob Lake was going into the Church,

being "the fool of the family," as Scamp Thorndyke had told Cecil Egerton up in the old walnut tree years before; and he was now very good-naturedly doing the office work in his father's business, which usually fell to Horace's share.

He had a hero worship for his elder brother, and would have done even a more unpleasant thing for his benefit.

Tom, the youngest of the family, was now at Sandhurst, an embryo officer, and in his cadet state was eagerly longing for his commission, and greater independence.

Lady Lynestone truly sorrowed for the kind old man who had done so much for her, but it was not a sorrow without hope.

Friends had quickly rallied around her, and now, no longer tied by her wifely duties to the side of her invalid husband, she mixed in a quiet way in the society of her acquaintances, daily becoming more admired and sought after.

Sir Richard and his household, in the shape of Adela and Lilian, had called upon the gentle widow, and a warm affection sprang up between the three ladies; but it was from Sir Richard's lips that Lady Lynestone learnt that her late lord's nephew and Adela's father had been close friends—a fact which drew her still nearer to the girl.

But, strange to say, Major Egerton was never spoken of between them.

Perhaps with some subtle insight into that mysterious thing, a woman's heart, the young widow guessed that there was a place in that of her new-made friend, Adela, a holiest of holies, into which none were invited to enter, and that the image there enshrined was Cecil Egerton's.

True it is that after the few first chance mentions of his name, she avoided it, or spoke of him with averted eyes, lest she should seem to watch the sad white face of the listener.

She told Cecil, in one of her letters, that she had made Adela's acquaintance, and how much she liked her; but her communication was not commented upon, and she wrote of her friend no more.

She was not of an inquisitive or interfering nature, and had no wish to pry into the feelings of those who showed no desire to make a confidante of her.

Cecil Egerton was eating his heart out in silent misery.

He would have given much for the information which he was too proud to seek, or even to encourage.

He could scarcely repress the longing to know all the particulars of Adela's supposed engagement, and yet he shrank from her very name.

He was for ever saying to himself that he

had put her outside his life, outside his love; but he left the door of his heart open for her to creep back and nestle there.

Mrs Thorndyke said little to her daughter of her father's health, and his own letters to her were cheery, and full of anticipation of a bright meeting, and Adela let her fears rest.

But the heart of the Rector's wife became heavier day by day, with a growing fear, and the family doctor was graver than of yore, for his patient's strength diminished instead of increasing.

He was advised to try change of air, but he shook his head.

"Home," he said, "was the place for a sick man, and he would stay there," nor would he hear of help in his work, his desire being to "die in harness."

It came with a shock to Adela, upon her return, to find her father so much weaker, and his pale cheeks so thin, but she smiled still in his presence, and he in hers, each keeping up the deception of hope for the other's sake.

She did not remain at Marsden Hall at all, but went straight home, blaming herself for her long absence, which had kept her from her duties of love.

Robert Lake was ordained, and a little plot was laid between the Rector's friends to give him help in spite of himself, and Mr Lake asked him as a personal favour to take his son as his curate.

He had a regard for the lad, and did not like to refuse, so the young man lived still with his parents, and lightened the Rector's work, doing the better from the fact that he felt all he did would save his senior, for whom he entertained a sincere esteem.

So the summer, to which Adela had looked forward, came, and was a bright one, but damped by her secret sorrow; and the new fear, which at first was only vague and shadowy, was now taking shape and form.

But still Mr Thorndyke was cheerful and active as his strength would allow.

He never spoke of his approaching end except to his wife, and from her he had never hidden the truth.

He had not guessed his daughter's love for Cecil Egerton, but he saw that his hopes as regarded Lord Carruthers were at an end. He had thought that meeting in Mentone, and being then thrown together, it was more than probable that Adela might learn to enjoy his society, and from that might grow fond of him; but upon learning from Sir Richard of his abrupt disappearance from among them, he could no longer shut the truth from his mind.

There was little doubt that Adela had

dismissed him again; and this opinion was shared by Sir Richard Freemantle, who was more at sea than ever to account for the trouble which he had at times surprised upon her face, the sorrow in her steadfast eyes.

When late autumn set in Mr Thorndyke found himself obliged to give up his clerical duties; but Bob Lake now knew all his ways, and daily conferred with him in his study, following out all his wishes.

And his friends looked hopefully forward to the spring to see the Rector better; and carefully his wife and daughter nursed him through the winter months.

Snow lay deep upon the ground, but no cold reached him in his snug home.

The holly, and the mistletoe, and the kind wishes of all around him, told him that it was Christmastide, and it pleased him to receive visitors for a little time, only he soon grew tired of listening and speaking.

Sir Richard seemed to have outgrown his delicacy, and there was no need for him to go abroad for his health or for pleasure. He felt he could not do so, with so much anxiety among his dearest friends.

Many and many a talk these two had together, for it was the Baronet's daily custom to drive over to the Rectory, and it was the greatest enjoyment of his life.

He missed Adela in his home more than he would have cared to confess, and the peep at her every twenty-four hours seemed to bridge over the gap in his existence occasioned by her absence.

Often and often he had it *au bout des lèvres* to ask the Rector if he would approve of his adopting his daughter in the future; but Mr Thorndyke had never spoken to him of his near end, and Sir

Richard was waiting for him to broach the subject, which he hoped he would one day do, but that hour never came.

It had always been the Rector's custom to read family prayers morning and evening, but the former was now delegated to his wife to do, for he was not able to get up till the middle of the day.

The evening devotion he still conducted before he went early to bed.

The winter had passed, and the first sudden warmth of the early spring days had begun, and Mr Thorndyke had found them unusually trying.

He had essayed to walk round his beautiful garden one day in the sunshine, but had been obliged to give up the attempt, from the unusual sensation of extreme weariness.

And he had rested placidly in his arm-chair, looking out towards the west, till the sun was sinking in bright effulgence in the sky.

"My dear," he said to Adela, who was sitting by his side, "I will read prayers now, and go to bed."

She looked at him in surprise.

"It is only six o'clock, father dear," she answered gently. "Did you forget the time? or will you have your dinner in bed to-night?"

"No, my child, I did not forget," he replied, in a faint voice; "but I am so tired, so weary; I want rest."

"Do not wait for prayers, darling!" she urged; "mother will read them. Let me give you my arm, and come at once."

"No," he answered, his eyes fixed upon the rosy west; "I will conduct them to-night."

Adela at once summoned her mother and the servants; and the Rector of

Winsthorpe read a few verses of the Bible, and prayed; and those who heard that short, earnest prayer never forgot it.

It was uttered in a low, sweet voice, and ended with a blessing. And Mr Thorndyke remained upon his knees, with bent head, the sun lighting up his pale face with seeming glory.

He did not move when the servants left the room, and Adela and her mother were very still, for the father and husband, as they thought, was still praying,—still kneeling there with closed eyes, and a peaceful smile upon his lips.

But Winsthrope's good pastor would neither preach, nor praise, nor pray any more on earth!

His weary body had found its needed rest. His spirit had fled to the Great Unknown, where the mystery of mysteries will be to each revealed.

CHAPTER IX.

THE NEW RECTOR OF WINSTHORPE.

THERE was scarcely a dry eye in Winsthorpe when the Rector, who had so long and so lovingly watched over them, was known to be dead.

He was mixed up in all that concerned both rich and poor.

He had buried their dead, comforted the mourners; he had given a strong hand over death's borderland to the feeble and dying; he had sat with the old, and read with them, and had ministered to the sick.

He had married the young men to the maidens, and baptised their children. He had known the secrets of many, and had faithfully kept them.

He had been true to his trust; a good shepherd, and the people of his flock knew it.

Most of them begged to be allowed to take one last look at the placid face, and not being refused, went, and laid their humble cottage flowers, bedewed with honest tears, at his feet; and the rare exotics which came after, were not more valued by the widow and orphan than the offerings of the poorer brethren who loved him.

There was no noise, no confusion, when they laid him in God's garden.

His followers were all mourners, not sightseers, and his mourners mourned him truly.

The funeral over, Sir Richard Freemantle drove to the Rectory.

"Mrs Thorndyke," he said kindly, taking both her hands in his. "I have come to fetch you and Adela. I have longed to do so every sad day of this sad week, but I felt that while *he* was here, nothing would entice you away."

"You were right," she answered, with tear-dimmed eyes. "I could not have gone, nor must you ask me just yet."

"For Adela's sake, if not for your own," he pleaded. "She is completely overwrought, utterly overdone!"

"For her sake I would do anything, but I do not think she would wish it. Every place is so dear here, because he loved them; there is not a thing which does not remind me of my darling."

"That is just it, you will never be better while you remain here."

"You must give me a little time," she said sadly. "I shall only have six weeks in my dear old home, then I must seek another. That is clerical law, I believe?"

"Well, will you promise to pay me a long visit then, since I cannot persuade you now?"

"Thank you, I shall be glad to do so. You are very kind."

"I am much disappointed," he replied. "I hoped to have carried you off tonight. Where is Adela?"

She heard his voice, and came down to him, pale and wan, a silent agony in her azure eyes, but no word of complaint rose to her lips, and Mrs Thorndyke had slipped away.

"Adela," he said softly, "my dear girl, my heart bleeds for you. I know what you have lost, but you must now let me be a father to you."

"No one can ever fill his place," she returned, in a low voice. "With me a place once filled in my affection is filled for ever!"

There was a look of keen disappointment upon the old Baronet's face; at the same time his admiration and respect for her increased.

"Then, my dear, I hope I may claim to be your friend?" he answered simply.

She stretched out her hand to him.

"One of my very best," she answered warmly. "It is good of you to come to us in our sorrow."

"My dear, I had hoped you would come to *me*. I desired to take you back with me, away from these sad memories."

"They are all we have," she said brokenly.

"Well, Adela, your mother would rather visit us later. Will that suit you?"

"I will do whatever she wishes," she returned wearily. "It seems so utterly sad for us to leave our dear old home?"

Sir Richard remained in deep thought

awhile, then there was a sudden brightening of his keen eyes, which showed an idea had struck him which had given him pleasure.

"May Lilian come to you to-morrow, child? She will be fairly vexed with me for not taking you home with me!"

"Mamma was right, our place is here for the present. Our time must needs be short, and there is much to be done."

"Will you mind leaving here very much?" he questioned.

"More than I can say. It has always been my home, and for mother the trial will be worse. I think this last straw will break her down. A clergyman's widow has always this last trouble above others, that however thoughtful her husband may have been, he cannot prevent her being turned from the home which has been her Eden."

"Well, well, child, do not meet troubles

half-way. Promise to come to me this day month and I will see what can be done with your dear father's successor. He may be in no hurry to take possession of the Rectory, you know it is in my gift."

"I had forgotten it, although I have heard both my parents speak most gratefully of your great kindness to them."

. . . .

So a month afterwards Adela Thorndyke and her mother were visitors at Marsden Hall, and Lilian and Sir Richard could not make enough of them.

"Horace," said the Baronet one day, "come and dine with me this evening, and bring your brother Bob with you. I have not forgotten that he did your work for you while we were at Mentone. He is a nice young fellow, and we must change him from a deacon into a priest as quickly as possible."

"He will be very pleased to accept your kind invitation, I am sure. He is fretting at the thought that he will have to leave here, poor old boy, but it is possible he might be re-engaged if you would recommend him to the new Rector."

"I'll see, lad, I'll see!" said Sir Richard. "You can both stay and talk to me when the ladies have retired this evening."

They did so; and the Baronet sat gazing upon the ground.

Suddenly he looked up.

"It seems like robbing the dead," he said, with emotion, "to put any one in dear old Thorndyke's place; but the living must be given away. Winsthorpe cannot be without a rector, so I mean to present it to the person who I think my poor friend would like best to see in his shoes, of whom I have heard him speak in warm terms."

"I quite understand your feelings, sir," replied the Curate. "It will be pain to me to see any other man in his pulpit, but I have grown fond of the people, and I should grieve to leave them. I have been hoping for your good word to the new Rector, if you think he is likely to require a helper."

"I don't think he is in the least likely to want one," replied the Baronet, with a smile, and a mischievous twinkle in his eyes. "He will be a strong young fellow, and able to do the work for himself."

The shadow of disappointment fell across Robert Lake's face.

"Then I am afraid there is but little chance for me," he said.

But Sir Richard did not seem to notice his remark.

He turned to Horace.

"Let me see—how old are you now?"

"I am twenty-five," he answered readily.

"And your brother?"

"Bob is three months over twenty-four; we came near together; Tom is considerably younger. By-the-bye, sir, he has got his commission."

"Has he? Well, he's a smart lad; he will make a good-looking soldier."

"His heart was set upon it. I'm very glad he has been able to follow his bent."

"Yours was the same way, my boy, was it not?" asked the Baronet.

"In years gone by, sir, but I am most thankful now that I remained here."

"Why?"

"For Lilian's sake."

"What, you don't believe in truth in absence?"

"Indeed I do, but we shall be much happier as it is."

"Yes! you are right, Horace; Lilian must have a settled home."

Suddenly he turned to Robert.

"Now, young man, what can I do for you?" he asked.

"For me, sir? Nothing, thank you," he stammered. "Had there been any chance of my being able to remain here, I would have asked you to help me in the matter, but as it is—"

"As it is, I owe you something for being a good-natured fellow, and doing your brother's work for nothing; and I want to get out of debt. Can't you think of any favour to ask?"

"I can't indeed."

"Humph! You're slow to seize an opportunity. Why don't you ask for the living for yourself, eh?" and Sir Richard looked at him keenly.

Robert Lake flushed.

"You are laughing at me, sir," he said

respectfully; "and, besides, I understood you had decided upon whom you mean to bestow it. Moreover, I am too young to solicit such favours, or to dream of such patronage."

"In fact you prefer being a curate? You're a perfect Tommy-too-good, eh, Master Bob? You're too young to see the advantages of having a living," laughed the Baronet.

"No, no. I'm not so young as that!" returned Bob, laughing too.

"Oh! not too young to *accept* a good living if ever it comes in your way, eh?"

"It is not likely to come in my way, sir!"

"I'm not so certain of that. Have you got your eye on a sensible wife, my boy? In my humble opinion, a parson should be a married man as well as a doctor."

The hot blood rushed into Bob Lake's face.

"Hallo! I see you have. Now, out with it. Who is the lady of your choice?"

"Really, sir—" he began.

"Nonsense! Let me hear if the lady is suitable; it's as much my business as yours."

"Excuse me, Sir Richard, but I really can't see that. If my heart has gone out to any one during the past few months, the fact is known only to myself."

"What, have you not told her? Men were not so cautious when I was young," chuckled the Baronet.

"What had I to offer, sir? And, besides," he added, growing crimson, "I have no reason to believe that she cares in the least for me. She is very gentle and kind, but I have noticed that she is so to the poorest man in the parish."

"In the parish!" repeated Sir Richard, regarding him intently. "You don't mean to say—"

"Bob!" cried Horace, "it's Adela. I see it all now. How I wish she would have you. Oh! shouldn't we all be happy?"

"I wouldn't ask her," blurted out poor Bob.

"Then it *is* Scamp!"

"I'm not ashamed to own my love for her, but, remember, I'm not going to tell her of it unless better times come, although in her trouble I have longed to ask her to let me comfort her, longed to shield her in some measure from the hard corners of life, which seem to grow sharper as troubles increase; but I will never ask a girl like Adela to undergo a life of poverty for my sake," he added, with feeling.

Sir Richard had been staring blankly at the speaker for some time. Then he rose, and paced the room with bent head and downcast eyes.

"If it could be, it would be best so," he murmured. "If ever I let another thought creep in, it was folly—folly, utter folly. It would settle the whole question. Yes; it would be best so!"

Suddenly he stopped by Bob's chair, and laid his hand kindly upon the young man's shoulder.

"My boy, *if* Adela loved you she would follow you to the world's end if you had not a penny in your pocket. She is a noble girl. I know none other like her —not even my own daughter. Still I respect your scruples, and poverty shall not stand in your way. As soon as you have taken priest's orders, and are *able* to hold it, the living of Winsthorpe shall be yours. I had intended this before I was aware of your adoration for my young favourite. Now I have double pleasure in bestowing it upon you. It would be a happy life for the dear girl to follow in the honourable and honoured footsteps of her parents. She loves the Rectory — every tree and shrub and flower. Every brick has a meaning for her beyond others. She will be glad to stay in her old home *if* she can care for you. If she does not, nothing will tempt her. In confidence, it was my intention that she and Mrs Thorndyke should not leave their beloved home. I meant to have given the old place to them, and to have built a new Rectory-house near the church. Should Adela accept you, this will become unnecessary, for I am sure you would not desire to part her mother from her, and I should expect you to give Mrs Thorndyke a suite of apartments for her own use, Mr Bob."

Robert Lake's colour came and went like a girl's, through his fair skin. He could not believe his own ears—could not believe that at twenty-four he was to hold a good living, to be able to ask Adela to be his wife, to offer her her dear old home, to remain near his own father and mother and Horace, and the people he had learnt to love!

He could scarcely find a word wherewith to thank his benefactor, but the Baronet liked him none the less for that fact.

"Do you really mean it, sir?" he faltered; "it seems all too bright for reality."

"I never say what I don't mean, lad," returned Sir Richard kindly; "so you may go home, and dream about it with safety."

"Bob, I congratulate you with all my heart!" cried Horace, seizing him by the hand, and shaking it as though its dislocation were his one object in life. "If only Scamp will say yes! but don't hope too much for *that*. Anyway, you're the luckiest young parson I know. Fancy your becoming the Rector of Winsthorpe at twenty-four! Won't Lilian be pleased?"

"I hope she will," said the Baronet, smiling.

"I think so. I wondered often she didn't ask the favour herself."

"None of us ever dreamed of such a piece of good fortune," said Horace. "And, Sir Richard, I don't know how to thank you for all your kindness to Bob, and to me too, during the last year and a half. It has been a truly happy time to me."

"Thank me by acts, lad, not by words. Continue to make my little girl as happy as you are now doing, and I shall be satisfied. I shall require no further proof of your gratitude; and, Horace, my boy, I have ceased to regret Lilian's choice. You're a good and honest fellow."

A sunbeam seemed to pass over the young man's face.

"Those are the best words I have ever heard in my life, sir!" he exclaimed, with emotion. "Next to when my darling confessed her love to me, I thought nothing could make me happier save the right to call Lilian my wife; but now I know that I was wrong, for you have lifted from my heart its last regret. In time, sir, I earnestly hope you will learn to regard me as a son."

"My lad, I do so already. Indeed, I have done so for a long time, but I have been too proud to acknowledge the fact, after my long opposition; but that dear girl's sweet sad face softened me, and I made up my mind I would tell you so to-night."

"You mean Adela's?"

"Yes, Horace. There is no other living face so sweet, and sad, and bright, by turns, and every mood seems to suit her best. I thought she never appeared so beautiful as she did to-night in her sable garments; her look was utterly *spirituelle!* If that young rascal gains her, he must be born under a lucky star indeed."

"I know it, sir, and I am not very hopeful *at present*," said Bob. "Adela may *in time* get to like me, but I am not very sanguine about it."

The old man shook his head.

"I don't believe in that sort of courtship, lad. Love is spontaneous. If she has no thought of you *now*, she never *will* have."

"Men have overcome even dislike, sir; and have gained the love they desire in the end," said Bob warmly.

"Perhaps! Better dislike than indifference. Moreover, they gain affection, not love, and it is not gained from such girls as Adela Thorndyke. There is nothing lukewarm about her. There *are* women who are little better than machines. They marry the first man who asks them, and one is as capable of making them contented as another."

"You are right, sir," said Horace. "If Adela does not really care for Bob, he may give it up at once. Time will never change her."

"I think, like myself, you understand her, my boy," said Sir Richard approvingly. "And now, young gentlemen, I've had enough of you both. Go home to bed, the pair of you. Robert, I wish you joy; and you, my lad, a continuance of it," as he gave Horace a bright nod and a slap on his shoulder.

Then he shook the young Curate's hand, and almost turned them out of the house.

"They are both good lads," he murmured, as he went upstairs to his bed-chamber, "and there is real pleasure in giving happiness."

"Papa, is anything the matter?" asked Lilian, fluttering out of her room in her pretty dressing-gown.

"Nothing, my child, except that you ought to be in bed and asleep," he said decidedly.

"I have been listening for Horace to go," she returned. "I never knew him stay so late after I had gone, and I feared something might be wrong."

"Ah! you thought you were the only attraction in the house, did you, lassie? and you may yet learn that you have to be jealous of your old father, for Horace and I are growing very fond of each other."

"I am so, so glad, father dear," she said softly, as she clung to his arm, and looked lovingly in his face. "He is a dear old fellow, is he not?"

"Yes, child, he's a good lad."

"And you don't wonder that I love him so dearly?"

"Not very greatly," he returned, with a smile, as he kissed her. "Go to bed, my dear. Where will your roses be to-morrow? Did you leave your friends comfortable?"

"Comfortable, yes! But oh! father, I cannot bear to look at Dela. She never says a word, but I really believe that her heart is breaking."

"Poor girl, poor girl, I wish I knew how to make her happy."

"And I."

"Lilian, are you in her confidence?"

"No, papa; and if I were, I could not betray it."

"Then we must pray to a higher power to help her, my dear; it is all we can do."

"Yes, I fear so!" replied Lilian sadly, and they bade each other good-night.

"Horace," said his brother, in a low voice, as they walked home side by side, "you have known Adela so long, do you think I have any chance?"

"'Faint heart never won fair lady,' old boy. She is worth trying for," returned he cheerfully.

"Ay! but you don't think she cares for me?"

"How on earth should I know?"

"You—you don't think she loves any one else?" he questioned anxiously.

"Would she be likely to tell me if she did?"

"I don't know; you have always been such friends, or Lilian might have told you."

"Neither Lilian nor Adela have told me anything, Bob, old boy; so you can but hope, and, remember, if Dela won't have you, there are as good fish in the sea as ever came out of it."

"Could you have comforted yourself with that idea, Horace, if Lilian had said no to you?" asked Robert, with a sad smile.

"No, Bob, I couldn't; and that's a fact."

"I thought not, no more can I," replied the other brokenly.

And the rest of the way the brothers walked on in silence.

In their father's hall they clasped hands.

"Don't lose heart, old boy," whispered Horace; "your can still hope."

"Yes, I can hope," returned the other, but he did not go up to bed with so light a heart as he ought to have done as the future Rector of Winsthorpe.

CHAPTER X.

SIR RICHARD'S RUSE.

ADELA, innocent of the affectionate adoration of the young Curate, so soon to be made Rector in her father's stead, received him in the kindliest spirit, fearing to damp his pleasure by seeming to grudge him the position which her own dear one could no longer hold.

Both she and Mrs Thorndyke were truly glad that the poor of Winsthorpe, who had so long been their care, should have so kind and good a pastor as Robert

Lake had proved himself to be during those trying months when Mr Thorndyke had been among them, and yet unable to attend to his duties.

He had shown both zeal and tact and patience, winning the good opinion of all around him; and they felt that it would be his pride to follow out all the plans and wishes of his predecessor, and to keep things going upon the same footing as they had been.

Adela warmly entered into all his thoughts and feelings about parish matters, and evinced more signs of life and energy than she had done since the blow fell, which had at the same time been both expected and unexpected.

She congratulated Sir Richard upon his wisdom in having selected Robert Lake, young though he was; and the Baronet smiled, sadly enough, but still he smiled.

Perhaps, after all, it was the young

Curate who had made a captive of the girl's heart, since it was not Lord Carruthers, as he had imagined; and of course, if so, his position, or the want of it, would fully account for there being no engagement between them, as well as for both the young people pining in secret.

And yet, good as Robert was, and honest and kind, he was scarcely the man Sir Richard would have pictured as the one to gain and enchain the heart of his favourite.

He felt that he should be more than glad when something should be settled.

In six months his promise to Lilian and Horace must be fulfilled. He must part from his child.

His mind was filled with half-formed desires, and shadowy resolves, concerning them both; but before he could really look the matter in the face, of one thing he was determined—to do his best to settle some future for Adela and her mother.

He would wait now until Winsthorpe's future Rector should plead his cause. If she should accept him, the matter would be soon arranged. If not, it was still left for him to see to their comfort, which as the Rector's old friend he would willingly have done, even if Adela had not been his beau ideal of living women.

But as it was, he felt it would be an equal pleasure to him to secure happiness to her as it would have been, had she been his own daughter.

Horace, looking on, felt hope for his brother grow.

Adela was so bright with him, so different from the pathetic-faced Adela whom he oft-times found when alone.

He spoke of it to Lilian, and the girl started.

"Robert loves our Dela!" she exclaimed,

in astonishment. "Well, poor old boy, I do not wonder. I wish she could fancy him, but if there were no other reason, I should imagine he is too young for her!"

"Why, Lil, there is only one year between us!" Horace returned.

"True, boy, but Bob is not you, you know," and she turned a pair of saucy, loving, brown eyes up to his face.

He stooped and kissed her.

"Little flatterer," he whispered; "but Bob is a better fellow than I am."

"It is quite right you should think so," she said, letting her hand wander among his warm, curly hair, while the smile deepened about her mouth; "but *I* know you're worth a dozen Bobs. Still he is a good boy too, as being your brother, he he could not fail to be; but, Horace, dear, it seems to me that Dela must have some one very out of the common—Lord Carruthers would have done for her."

"Evidently she did not think so," returned Lilian's lover mischievously, "for she certainly could have had him if she had so desired."

"That is true," she acknowledged reluctantly.

"Now, pet, cannot you suggest someone else who is more suited to her than poor old Bob?" continued Horace quizzically.

She remained in thought for awhile then she looked up at him with a sudden brightness.

"Horace, do you remember Major Egerton?"

"What! the old young man who surprised me giving Scamp a letter for you in the tent! who glared at me so murderously that I began to think he was a rival for your hand, darling! Oh yes, I have not forgotten him, and a precious disagreeable-looking fellow I thought him."

"Nonsense, dear; he was an eminently handsome man, a symphony in autumn tints, a picture man! and a brave fellow to boot."

"Well! all I can say is, he must have looked at you with a very different expression of countenance to that with which he honoured me. I thought him *diabolical!*" he retorted dogmatically.

"Green eyes!" laughed Lilian. "Major Egerton is undeniably handsome; but you would never think any one good enough for Dela, if it came to the point."

"Yes, I should. I would like to see her Bob's wife muchly."

"Of course; then she would be your sister, you old sinner. But I tell you that poor old Bob will never gain her."

"I am sorry for it. The disappointment will go near to breaking his heart!" Then he added suddenly,—"Lilian, if you know anything, it will be only right to speak.

If Adela is already engaged, we must not let poor old Robert make himself ridiculous."

"No, she is not engaged, dear!" replied Lilian sadly; "of that I am certain, but more I cannot say."

Horace had felt a little ruffled that Lilian should place any other before his brother as more eligible for the hand of his old playmate, but it quickly wore off, and he said warmly,—

"Well, pet, watch them together. No one arouses Adela from her lethargy like Bob after all, and I think he *has* a chance."

Lilian did watch them, and was bound to confess that Horace was right.

Was it possible that Dela had forgotten? Had she really determined to let the past rest and go into oblivion, and to attempt a new path in life?

She knew how she loved her old home,

and might not the fact that if she could care for Bob she need never leave it, be an inducement to her to accept the new Rector for her husband?

If even Adela's best friends began to look upon the alliance as possible, need it be wondered at that, hope increased in the heart of her lover?

He hovered about her path. He brought her every scheme, every plan and thought, in connection with Winsthorpe, to ask her advice and learn her wishes upon it. And Adela, remembering only what her father would have desired, entered into it all for his dear sake, little understanding the construction which was being put upon her conduct.

And so things went on, but Bob never found himself sufficiently at home with her to plead his cause, and day by day the Baronet interrogated him with word or look, to receive the same answer.

"I have never had the chance, sir."

"Chance!" repeated Sir Richard warmly. "When I was young, men made opportunities, now they expect them arranged for them. Very well, young man, *I* must find you the chance, I suppose. Come here to lunch to-morrow, and leave the rest to me."

So it turned out that the next morning the Baronet sat down beside Adela for a talk. Robert Lake had been asking his help for a labourer, living some miles distant, upon the very borders of the parish, upon whom some timber had fallen, rendering the poor fellow perfectly helpless.

He had been carried to his poor home, and had lain there for a month past in an abject state of suffering and poverty, his wife being unable to leave him and her large family of little ones, to go out to earn anything.

"Adela," said Sir Richard, "something must be done for that poor fellow Jenkins, his case is a pitiable one. Suppose we drive over and see him this afternoon?"

"With pleasure, dear Sir Richard," she answered readily. "It is so little I can do now, I am no longer in the groove to be of use to any one. I shall be only too glad to go with you!"

"Well, well, who knows how soon a life of usefulness may again be yours, my dear? At any rate, we will see what we can do to-day."

END OF VOL. II.

COLSTON AND COMPANY, PRINTERS, EDINBURGH.

www.ingramcontent.com/pod-product-compliance
Lightning Source LLC
Chambersburg PA
CBHW022011220426
43663CB00007B/1039